Seasons of Change

Meeting the Challenge of a Nursing Home

Jeri Lee-Hostetler

BRETHREN PRESS
Elgin, Illinois

Seasons of Change
Meeting the Challenge of a Nursing Home

Copyright © 1988 by JERI LEE-HOSTETLER

BRETHREN PRESS, 1451 Dundee Avenue, Elgin, Illinois 60120

Cover design by Vista III

Library of Congress Cataloging-in-Publication Data

Lee-Hostetler, Jeri.
    Seasons of change.

    1. Basinger, Louisa Nussbaum, 1869-1975—Fiction.
I. Title.
PS3562.E3664S43   1988   813'.54   88-5022
ISBN 0-87178-774-1

Manufactured in the United States of America

Contents

Author's Note   v
1. Good-by 1
2. And Hello 9
3. Louisa Herself. 19
4. Heartaches 27
5. Early Memories 37
6. Amos 47
7. Chris 63
8. My Children . . . My Friends 71
9. Losing a Best Friend 85
10. A Lower Gear 95
11. Roommates 104
12. Johnny. 118
13. The Fight 132
14. Jessie Leaves, Johnny Returns 143
15. Not Really Louisa. 152
16. This I Was, This I Am 161
17. And the Children Cried 175
18. Louisa Goes Home 184

TO TERI,
who knows how to love an outcast.

And to the memory of our great-grandmother,
LOUISA NUSSBAUM BASINGER,
who knew what it was to be an outcast.

AUTHOR'S NOTE

This is a story of fact and fiction, of truth brought to life by imagination. It is based on the life of Louisa Nussbaum Hochstetler Basinger of Pandora, Ohio, my great-grandmother.

When Louisa Basinger died, those of us who loved her shared a lot of stories. Her children and grandchildren have always told stories about her, I guess. But after her death, there was a time when someone always seemed to be talking about memories.

Many of the incidents in the story are true. The setting is the Swiss Mennonite community of Bluffton-Pandora in northwest Ohio. Gramma was born on March 28, 1869. Not long after that, her father developed his habit of leaving the family now and then, and on such occasions, her mother placed the children with local farmers to work for room and board.

Gramma married Amos Hochstetler on May 23, 1889. The houses in Beaverdam and Lima in which they lived were much as I have described them. To them were born four children, three boys and a girl. Their divorce in 1903, the move back to Pandora with the three older children, her alienation from the Mennonite tradition, the times of sending the children to bed hungry, these things are all part of the stories I heard.

When Gramma was about fifty years old, she married Chris Basinger, and the two of them lived for nearly fifty happy years in a little house on Monroe Street in Pandora.

When she was nearly ninety-nine years old, Gramma's children moved her and Chris to a nursing home. In that home, Gramma and Chris celebrated their fiftieth wedding anniversary, just before Chris died.

From the day in 1886, when Gramma—as she put it—"was converted," she walked in faith. Although severely tested, her faith never faltered. And on July 5, 1975, at the age of 106, Gramma Basinger finally went home.

As I added to my collection of memories stories from friends and relatives, the idea took shape that her story should be preserved. This book is the result.

Most of the characters in the story are real people, but almost all of the names have been changed. Basically, the changes are symbolic of the fact that my imagination has been at work. Because my imagination has touched the events of Gramma's life and the people associated with her, I let it touch their names also.

Most of the place names are correct. However, there is no Parmenter County or Parmenter County Nursing Home in Ohio. I suppose anybody who really wanted to could find out the name of the nursing home where my great-grandmother spent the last years of her life. For that reason, I must state that Parmenter County Nursing Home, its staff and its residents are purely creations of my imagination, although I have found such people and such conditions in other places where the elderly are cared for.

As for the story as a whole, I know this isn't exactly how it was. But knowing Gramma, her love for God and her deep faith, this is how it might have been. Any faulty interpretation of her life is clearly my own.

My sincere thanks to everyone who helped with research for this project: to the grandchildren who told the stories; to Eli G. Steiner, to Delbert Gratz, Elizabeth Baringhaus Battingly, and Ralph E. Waite, Jr.; to my grandfather, the late Harry Hostetler, Louisa's son, and to his wife, Alice; and to my cousin, Teri Schaefer, who was where I could not be to ask questions and check on details.

Jeri Lee-Hostetler
Battle Ground, Washington

1

GOOD-BY

When Louisa awoke, she had forgotten what day it was. There were robins in the cherry tree outside her bedroom window, perking their way from branch to branch, all atwitter with the joy of morning and a fine day ahead. Warm sunshine sparkled through lace curtains to pattern the far wall and the faded picture that hung there—Christ, knocking at the door.

Life seemed so fine.

A soft, pleasant snoring caught her ear, and Louisa turned to look across the room at Chris. All she could see of him was a small, motionless lump in the other bed with a bush of tousled, gray hair peeking out at the top of the covers.

Handsome, he was. "It isn't," she thought, "just that I remember the way he used to be. He's *still* handsome. Still the finest Christian gentleman I ever met."

He stirred then, under the wedding ring quilt, and her fingers brushed each other softly, as if caressing a fine piece of fabric. She loved that quilt. It was one of the finest she had ever made, and it seemed that she could feel it still in her hands and in this way remember the joy of piecing it in celebration of their twenty-fifth wedding anniversary.

But that was long ago. Today was today—and somehow she still had not caught the dreadful significance of it.

Familiar lumps in her old cotton mattress were as comfortable as a gathering of old friends. Louisa stretched and threw back the covers. Lying there quietly in a shapeless flannel nightgown, she felt ready for the day of hard work that she thought lay ahead of her.

It would be a good day to bake bread. As soon as the idea came, she could feel her fingers deep in the soft dough, kneading.

And the warm, crusty loaves. She could smell the aroma drifting from her oven through the screen door to mingle with the scented air of spring and the roses by the back porch.

Or pie. Pie would be good, too. Maybe better. Chris loved cherry pie, and she could use the last of the canned cherries from summer, and be ready for the new when they came on.

Somehow the new ones always tasted better if the old ones were used up first—or given away.

Then, in delighted anticipation of the things she would accomplish, Louisa moved—and truth began to break over her like an angry dawn.

It was a struggle just to sit up. When she did, she saw in the mirror on the bureau across the room the old woman she had forgotten.

That old woman stared back with a face that was pleasant, but deeply lined, and yellow-white hair that hung in a long braid down her back.

Louisa believed that a proper woman wore her hair long, and for fifty years or more no scissors had come close to that braid. She was very proud of it.

The old woman's eyes—Louisa reached for her glasses and put them on—had once been a brilliant blue, but had faded with nearly a century of use. The hands that lingered beside the glasses were gnarled and bent, mapped with random lines of dark, raised veins.

Then Louisa remembered.

For a brief moment she wondered if she would cry. Her eyes were dry, but her heart seemed almost overwhelmed with tears. There would be no cherry pies today. No bread, either.

Because it was the day.

Years before, she had wondered if such a day would ever come to her. She had feared it and had hated the very thought of it. Now it was here.

She looked at the clock, leaning close to be sure she saw the numbers right. Six-thirty. At ten o'clock, Wallace and Mary would be there to take her away.

She had lived in that house half a century. Every room, every crack in the linoleum, every leak in the ceiling was home to her. There were only three and one-half hours left to live there.

But I still have those three and a half hours, she thought. *No one can take them away from me—not until I've lived through them, held them close to my heart, and made their memories mine forever.*

It was feeble comfort. Three and one-half hours were so terribly short, compared to fifty years.

Perhaps, she thought, *if I just go about my business and pretend it isn't going to happen, it will be easier.* She reached out with a trembling hand and turned the clock to the wall.

Getting out of bed was a struggle, too. The change from lying down to standing always brought its moment of dizziness. In a second or so, it would pass—but for those seconds, she had to be careful not to fall.

She put on her robe and slippers. Then, bracing herself against the bed, the chest of drawers, the wall, she made her way to the bathroom. The weakness surprised her, as it did every morning. *I seem to be shaky today,* she thought.

When she came back, Chris was awake, peering at her from beneath the covers.

"Don't you think," he said, "that you ought to use your walker?"

At the word, Louisa's eyes snapped toward the mass of tubing at the foot of the bed, as though it were magnetized. She had forgotten it was there. "I suppose I ought," she said. "I seem to be shaky today."

Chris accepted that, and Louisa took the walker and clumped off in the direction of the kitchen.

She would like to have dressed before they came. But dressing was such a chore, and it took so long.

When it first became difficult for her to dress herself, there had been friends who dropped in to help. After that,

Wallace and Mary had hired a girl who came off and on through the day to help with things like dressing and meals. Now there was nobody. Wallace told her she had been too cross with all of them. It was one reason they were going to take her away.

Don't think about that, she reminded herself.

She would like to have prepared one last meal on the old cast-iron gas cook stove with its speckled enamel doors. But she was not supposed to. They didn't want her to.

"It's too much for you these days, Ma," Wallace had said, squinting at her from behind thick, wire-rimmed glasses.

"Humph!" snorted Louisa. "I'll show that young whippersnapper what's too much for me!"

Rolling up the sleeves of her robe and gown, she turned on the burner beneath a heavy iron skillet and began a breakfast of bacon and eggs with coffee and leftover pie.

By the time the smell brought Chris, dressed and shuffling, to the table, everything was almost ready. He set their favorite dishes on the red-and-white checked oilcloth—brown earthenware for himself, a pattern of blue cornflowers for Louisa—and the two of them sat down to say a quiet blessing: "Lord," Chris said, "bless this food and bless the hands that prepared it."

"Amen," from Louisa.

They ate in silence.

Louisa made it a point to cherish every bite. She did enjoy good food. It might be the last time for a long time they would have a breakfast like that. *I know what breakfast in those places is like,* she thought. *It's like in a hospital: cold mush; cold, greasy toast with a dab of jelly; lukewarm coffee.*

She shook her head. The bacon and egg sat mellow on her tongue, and the hot, black coffee felt good all the way down.

Chris pushed back his chair. "I'd like another cup, if it's convenient," he said softly and smiled at her as she poured.

When they had finished, Louisa hobbled to the sink with her walker and ran water for the dishes.

A whole lifetime of dishwashing ended that day. It was an odd feeling—to know that she would never again plunge her hands into steaming, soapy water to scrub at a spot of dried egg or oatmeal.

Taking time to love each of the dishes, she dried them with a soft, embroidered cloth. There were two fuzzy bear cubs holding a banner with the word, "Monday" on it. One of her great-grandchildren had made it years ago. Louisa reached carefully up to put each one in its own place in the cupboard for the last time. Closing the door upon them, she turned away when the idea came. *Well, why not?* she thought. *They're mine.*

Her best-loved dishes came back out of the cupboard and into a brown paper bag which Louisa carried to her room to set beside a partly-packed suitcase. She would take them with her. The thought filled her with a warm and comfortable joy.

Chris by that time had moved into the front room to spend his last minutes at home in his favorite rocker.

Louisa could not sit. There was a restlessness inside her which drove her and the walker clumping around the house on a farewell tour.

Clump. A flock of sparrows flitted upward from the sill as Louisa passed the kitchen window. The whisper of their wings seemed to her a lonely sound, and it reached out to brush her heart with sorrow.

"I love those little fellows," Chris had always said of the sparrows.

It had been a long time since she or Chris had unlocked the screen to reach out and scatter crumbs on the feeding tray there. Yet they still waited, tiny, patient, feathered balls of hope and trust.

"Good-by," Louisa said to them as they settled back to hope once more. "Good-by, small friends. I'll miss you."

Clump. Clump. The huge oak buffet in the dining room. A wedding present from her father and mother, she had used it for eighty years. *Good-by.*

Clump. A whole roomful of crisp doilies, antimacassars and table cloths she had crocheted. *Good-by.*

Clump. Clump. At the front window, Louisa stopped to look across Monroe Street at the houses of the neighbors opposite. *Good-by.*

Tom Shandy was out mowing his lawn with one of those horrible, noisy power mowers. She remembered when he was just plain Tommy and used to push the softly-whirring hand mower every Saturday morning—then stop by afterwards, sweating, to trade conversation for a couple of cookies and some milk. *Good-by, Tommy.*

It was garbage day. Up and down the street strange things sat by the curb—boxes of grass clippings from fresh spring lawns; shiny new trash cans and battered old ones; giant green plastic bags that bulged or ripped; two houses down, a worn, ancient chair that someone was throwing away.

Ausgespielt, she thought. *Like me.*

There was a time when a chair that good would have been repaired and proudly used. There was a time when an old woman . . .

A gleaming blue Ford intruded on her vision and her thoughts. Wallace and Mary had arrived.

Suddenly Louisa needed to sit down, but the closest chair was too far away. Gripping the walker hard, she fought for strength to remain upright.

Tears blurred her view as she watched them get out of the car to start up her front walk.

Dear Jesus, Louisa thought, *couldn't I just die now? . . . here? . . . this morning? Without having to leave?*

From behind her came the sound of choking. Chris had seen them, too. Louisa turned in time to catch him wiping tears with the back of one leathery hand.

Resentment, harsh and bitter, rose in Louisa. *I wonder,* she thought, *if I hate them for doing this to us.*

Wallace poked his head in the door. "Hi, folks," he said. "Anybody home?"

"Not for long," muttered Louisa, and turned away from him.

Mary came then, a warm smile in the deep blue eyes, the color that Louisa's own eyes had once been. Mary, who had been friend as much as daughter, was, in the pain of the moment, no longer friend but stranger, a demanding woman whom Louisa had never seen before.

Mary's smile faded as she sniffed suspiciously at the left-over smell of bacon and eggs and coffee. Her shoulders stiffened. "Well," she said, "I guess we don't have to take you out for breakfast after all."

It was over quickly. By eleven o'clock, Louisa was dressed. The white hair that hung nearly to her feet had been let down and combed, then braided and wrapped neatly around her head again and they were both packed.

Mary snapped the locks on the two tiny suitcases—that was all they were allowed to take at first—and set them on the floor. "Are we about ready to go?"

"Yes," said Louisa, reaching for her purse and for her dishes in the brown paper bag.

"What's that?" demanded Mary.

"Just a dish or two I'm taking along," Louisa answered, hugging the bag to her.

But Mary already had her hands on the sack and was unrolling the top of it. Peering in, she exclaimed, "Mother!" The word was thick with impatience. "You can't take these."

"Why not, I'd like to know!"

"Because," Mary explained as if she were talking to a child, "everything like that is supposed to be provided for you." She pried the sack from Louisa's grip and set it back on the bed. "I think we'd better get going."

Louisa's eyes narrowed thoughtfully. "I need to use the bathroom first," she announced.

Mary picked up the two suitcases and walked toward the front room. "I'll wait for you out here," she said over her shoulder.

Louisa unrolled the top of the brown paper sack and reached in. Dismay raced through her for one awful moment when her hand trembled, and the dishes clinked together. But the others were talking and did not hear.

Slowly, quietly, Louisa drew her small breakfast bowl out of the bag and hid it in the bottom of her purse.

Straightening, she drew a deep breath. "I'm ready!" she called.

Louisa turned to look back at her yard as long as it could be seen. It wasn't much. The grass was shaggy with lots of dandelions but lots of roses and fruit trees as well.

"I'm going to miss those roses," she said, not quite sure that she had spoken aloud.

"Me, too," said Chris, sighing.

"Oh, Ma," said Wallace. "Don't even think about those old things. There'll be lots nicer roses where you're going."

A twenty-five minute drive through tiny villages and rolling farm country brought them to their destination. The blue Ford eased into a long driveway. There was a quick impression of haughty brick buildings; sculptured, well-manicured lawns; bark dust and bushes heavy with flowers, as they pulled in front of the entrance.

"Parmenter County Nursing Home," said the words above the door. Little words below added, "Specializing in the finest care for the aged and infirm."

When Wallace helped her from the car, Louisa stopped and read and pondered.

What will it be like, she asked herself, *to spend the rest of my life in the shadow of such words?*

Holding her head high and leaning on Wallace's arm, Louisa hobbled through the door.

2

AND HELLO

As soon as they were inside the green and gold reception area, a nurse in a white uniform came running with a wheelchair. "Hello," she said, formally. This one was a stickler for duty. "I'm Mrs. Whitehead." She plunked Louisa into the chair and pointed her toward the admissions desk.

Riding was *easier* than walking. There was no denying that. For the past several years, Louisa had been having trouble with the floor when she walked. It always seemed to be trying to rearrange itself beneath her. One minute it was right under her foot as she stepped forward. By the next step it might be lower—or higher—than she had expected, and she would have to catch herself awkwardly or fall.

But riding was not more *pleasant* than walking.

Louisa would like to have stalked up to the desk under her own power and announced, "Well, I'm here."

Instead, they wheeled her over the thick carpet. Chris tried to follow. At eighty-nine, he was nearly ten years younger than Louisa, and he clung fiercely to his ability to do for himself.

For years he had walked daily to the post office, ten slow blocks, to sit on the bench outside with his cronies, soaking up sunshine and cackling laughter before he brought the mail home to her.

When had he stopped doing that? Oh yes. Right after the first time she fell.

She had been sitting on a stool and started to get up. The floor had gone out from under her, and the stool had turned over.

"Oh, my dear . . . my *dear*!" Chris had said. Hobbling to her, he had tried to help, but his frightened, futile efforts did nothing to ease the pain.

When she came home from the hospital, he had stopped making his daily trip to town. After that, neighbors brought the mail.

Now an aide came with a wheelchair for Chris, too. He shook off her hand and clambered in by himself, seeming not so much angry as faintly saddened by this new attack on his dignity.

Like two ancient babies in chrome and green canvas carriages, they were wheeled away.

The admissions desk was elbow height—a convenient leaning place for a person standing up. It was impossible for Louisa to see over the thing. She would have stood, but a firm, gentle hand on her shoulder kept her in place.

"Now," said a scratchy female voice, and there was the sound of paper being rolled into a typewriter. "We have several forms to fill out. Please answer each question as briefly as possible."

Wallace and Mary came close to the desk.

"We'll begin with your mother first," said the voice. "What is her name?"

"Louisa Basinger," Mary said, while the keys on the typewriter began to peck at the paper.

"Louisa *Nussbaum* Basinger," said Louisa, "and I can answer my own questions." Chris nodded in vigorous agreement.

The typewriter stopped, and behind the desk, a chair scraped back. Reproving gray eyes in a pinched face leaned over to inspect Louisa. "That is *not*," said the voice, "how we usually do it." A stern mouth was turned to smile at Wallace and Mary.

"Well, it *is*," said Louisa, "how we are doing it this time." But she did not turn—and she did not smile.

The eyes looked again, frustrated, to Wallace and Mary, hoping for an argument. When none was forthcoming, a frown replaced the smile. The face disappeared; the chair scraped again.

Wallace wandered off across the lobby. Mary stayed.

The voice behind the desk started down a list of questions. Most of them seemed so impertinent that Louisa thought about refusing to answer. But if she didn't reply, Mary would.

Is the patient accustomed to bathing himself? Dressing himself? Feeding himself?

Is he continent? For a moment, Louisa couldn't think what that one meant. . . .

Does he require glasses? Hearing aid? False teeth . . . or any other prosthetic device? Please specify.

What serious illnesses has the patient had?

"Mostly I am a healthy woman," answered Louisa. "And I consider myself blessed to be that way."

"Answer the question, please," said the voice.

"Well," said Louisa, "I had typhoid fever once." "I was a young woman then, with two children. The fever forced me to have a doctor. He gave me turpentine! I guess you could say that after that I never got sick enough to call a doctor. That stuff tasted so terrible that I wouldn't have another doctor near me until I knew they had newer methods to use."

A sigh came from behind the desk, and Louisa could almost hear the typist raise her eyes to heaven and shrug her shoulders in dismay. Somehow, it felt good.

"Does the patient often fall? Has he ever had a *serious* fall?"

"No," said Louisa. "No . . . no . . . no!"

"Mother!" said Mary.

They eyed each other warily for a long moment. Louisa was the first to drop her eyes. "Well, I got over it, didn't I?" she grumbled.

"*Them*, Mother. You got over *them* . . . and not very well." Then Mary launched into an account of why Louisa and Chris needed to be in the nursing home.

Louisa *did* fall. They could no longer take care of themselves. It was impossible in this day and age to get someone to come in to cook and clean for them or help out. Both of them needed nursing care. They couldn't even keep themselves *clean* any more. They almost always spilled food on the front of their clothes. Their hair . . . and their fingernails. . . . Her voice carried a trace of disgust which Louisa pretended not to notice.

Mrs. Whitehead still stood behind Louisa's wheelchair listening politely. *Can eyes yawn?* thought Louisa, when she twisted her head and shoulders to look up at the nurse. Somehow the woman's eyes seemed to be yawning at Mary's outburst.

I wish I could go home, thought Louisa. *We're hardly even here yet, and I really want to go home.*

Wallace had been in conversation with a woman patient across the lobby. Smiling, he broke away from her suddenly and bustled toward them, looking important.

"Say," he turned from one member of the staff to another—receptionist, nurse, aide—not quite knowing whom to address. "This lady says she would like to have a cup of coffee with some cream substitute." He grinned and winked at the three women, as if all of them were conspiring about something. "She says she's already got some sugar substitute, so I don't need to get any of that."

There was an awkward pause. "Uh," said Wallace, "where could I find some?"

Mrs. Whitehead sighed heavily. "No," she said, pursing her lips and shaking her head. "No, she's not allowed to have coffee. She tries that with everyone who is new around here—but she is *not allowed to have it!*" She spoke the last words as though Wallace had been incredibly foolish to believe a patient.

"Oh," said Wallace. A warm glow of embarrassment ran up his cheeks. He turned and walked away, importance drained from him.

The voice behind the desk drew their attention back to the papers, and they finished the impertinent questions—first for Louisa, then for Chris.

"Now, are there any other items of particular importance which we need to know?"

"Yes," said Louisa. Heads swiveled toward her, expectantly. "I want to go home."

"Mother!" There was new frustration in the word every time Mary said it.

When Louisa turned to her daughter, there were tears in Mary's eyes, and a brief, grim compassion swept painfully through Louisa's heart. She reached out to her, patting the gentle hand only twenty years younger than her own.

"I know, dear," said Louisa, sighing. "This *is* difficult for you." She sank back into her chair and was silent.

"Ahem!" The receptionist cleared her throat and rattled her pencils. "We need," she said, "a list of personal possessions which the patient is bringing into the home."

"They forget sometimes, you know," she whispered loudly to Mary. "This way. . . ."

Louisa pretended not to hear.

Mary nodded understanding and reached into her pocket. "Right here," she said. "I made a list for you when I finished the two suitcases this morning."

The receptionist was standing now to receive the list. Her stapler banged, attaching the list to the other papers. The eyes in the pinched face surveyed them all, then fell to Louisa's lap.

"What about her purse?" asked the receptionist, gesturing toward the scuffed black handbag over Louisa's arm, as though Louisa were not there.

"Oh, no!" Louisa clutched it to her as if it were a part of her own body they were trying to tear from her. "No! You can't have my purse."

But they had it. As if it were not really hers at all, the surgery was done, and the purse was in their hands.

"You see," said the receptionist, holding up the little cornflower cereal bowl in triumph. "It often happens. They try to slip something extra in like this, then I get in trouble for letting them do it."

She rummaged quickly through the bottom of the purse, snapped it shut and handed the bowl to Mary with a saccharine smile. "You won't need it, honey," she said to Louisa. "We provide all dishes and utensils."

Louisa felt strangely as if the woman had reached out and slapped her.

"Take them into the day room," instructed the receptionist, "while I get signatures here and settle final details."

The nurse behind Louisa and the aide behind Chris gave the handles a shove, and the chairs rolled again, carrying the two of them deeper into the confines of the building, Louisa first, Chris following.

"What about my signature?" Louisa wondered loudly as they started.

"I'm sorry, honey." That "honey" was starting to grate, like cracker crumbs in a clean bed. "We don't need yours—just your children's."

I'll bet you're sorry, thought Louisa. *And I wouldn't give it to you if you did need it—not without a fight. So there!*

They passed an old man in a flannel shirt, baggy pants, and gray suspenders. He was wandering around calling softly, "Where's my room? . . . Where's my room?"

They passed other empty-eyed residents in wheelchairs, propelling themselves aimlessly through the corridors.

One woman had the footrest on her chair folded up. A woven strap around her hips held her in the chair as she scooted along, pulling herself with her feet. While she scooted, she wailed, "Untie me . . . Won't somebody please untie me. . . . Untie me . . . ," in an endless refrain.

This first confrontation with people who were expected to become her companions and new friends left Louisa feeling weak. She turned to look around the nurse at Chris, needing assurance that he was still there and that everything was still well with him.

His lips trembled sadly until he saw that she was looking, and then he tried to smile. She would have spoken some encouragement to him—but there did not seem to be anything to say.

"Ahh," said Mrs. Whitehead, turning into the day room, "here we are." It was a large, well-lighted room, with picture windows looking out over a handsome view of farmland and orchards and an occasional field of Holsteins, black and white spots on a grassy quilt. Around the room were lines of chairs and wheelchairs. Some lines were straight, where attendants had arranged them while others were staggered, where residents had done their own arranging.

"This is the day room," the nurse went on. "It's kind of like a living room. Most of our people spend some time here every day. See. . . ." She directed Louisa's attention with a pointing finger. "Aren't the flowers pretty?"

"Yes," replied the aide, pulling up beside them with Chris. "They certainly are. Look, there are three different arrangements."

"My, they are nice." It was the nurse again.

The conversation ended as Louisa's chair was shoved into the line-up. The woman next to Louisa caught the last sentence or so.

"Humph!" snorted the woman, leaning close to Louisa as soon as the nurse and the aide walked away. "Humph! You know where those flowers are from, don't you?"

Louisa turned to examine the arrangements more closely. Suddenly she knew what was coming.

"They're from the *mortuary,* that's where," said the woman. "And I don't like 'em." She shuddered. "I wish they didn't bring them from there!"

Well, thought Louisa, *maybe it's appropriate.*

"I think it's in awfully poor taste," said the woman, nearly whimpering, "to bring them from there."

Louisa looked around the room, studying the line-up. Most of the people were staring at a color TV at one end of the room. She turned away. Louisa didn't like TV.

The real people were more interesting, anyhow, in an appalling sort of way.

A woman who had obviously dressed herself shuffled away from them, out the door. Her clothes were on backwards, and her shoes were on the wrong feet.

Attached to another woman's wheelchair was a bag made of heavy plastic, with a tube draining into the bag. The bag looked as if it were half full of urine. The woman's fingers plucked endlessly at the twists in the tube. Her vacant eyes indicated that she was not aware of the plucking.

"Continent . . ." the word the receptionist had said came roaring back at Louisa, and suddenly she remembered what it meant.

A balding man who had long ago been a giant huddled in an easy chair. His hands were still the hands of a worker—rough and holding traces of the power that had once been in them. As he sat staring into space, now and again the hands reached out, as if looking for work they should be doing: a hammer to hold, a motor to tinker with, a strong son's arm to grip. The rest of him had adjusted to his age—but the hands had never got used to being idle.

One resident might have been a robot. Her voice was tinny and flat. With every word at precisely the same pitch, she raged at the attendants. "I . . . want . . . something . . . to . . . eat . . . right . . . *now!*" she demanded. "Bring me something to eat *now!* Bring me something to cover my legs *now!*" Bring . . . me . . . something . . . to . . . cover . . . my . . . arms . . . *now!*" Periodically, as they all ignored her, the woman would begin a flood of the vilest cursing Louisa had ever heard.

"God . . . damn . . . you!" And much more. "Bring . . . me . . . something . . . to . . . eat . . . *now!*"

"Oh, dear Lord, let your name be blessed," whispered Louisa, almost as an involuntary reaction to the oath. It was as if her blessing might blot out the cursing of the other woman, somehow making everything right for the God she loved.

Behind Louisa and Chris, a shrunken man muttered the alphabet over and over, repeating the letters as though they were words in some long and fascinating sentence. Each time he came to Z, he started over. Sometimes, for variety, he would count to ten or throw in a nonsense sentence for good measure. "A . . . B . . . C . . . D . . . *E* . . . It tried to jump all by itself . . . A . . . B . . . C . . . D . . . E . . . G . . . 1 . . . 2 . . . 3 . . . 4 . . . It has an A . . . B . . . C . . . ."

At the west door of the day room, an aide looked in and waved at two women in adjoining chairs, before going back out again. "Hi, you two cutie-wooties," said the aide. Grins in matching, wrinkled faces showed matching sets of toothless gums.

Dear God, thought Louisa, *is that going to be how they talk to us here?*

Suddenly there was a hand on Louisa's arm, and she turned, startled, to find a bewhiskered woman leaning close, peering into her face. "You know, you hurt my mother's feelings awful bad . . . what you said the other day."

Louisa stared at her, dumfounded. "I've never *seen* you before," she said. "I don't know your mother."

"Oh," said the other. "Then it must have been us who hurt you." There were tears beginning to sparkle in the ancient eyes, and the whiskery chin was trembling. "Do you have any bad feelings toward us? Can you forgive us?"

Louisa turned to look at Chris, to see how he was taking it all. He sat slumped in his wheelchair, chin on chest, eyes closed in a posture of total surrender.

While she was watching him, Wallace and Mary arrived with another nurse. "We're ready to move you to your room, now," the nurse announced, taking the handles of Louisa's chair and whirling it about.

Mary grabbed Chris's chair and followed.

Wallace had the suitcases.

In the hall they passed a gaudy bulletin board where bewildered faces in party attire peered from colored snapshots as though they were waiting perpetually for someone to explain what was going on.

A few feet past the central nurses' station, they turned right. Louisa became aware of an unpleasant odor that grew stronger and stronger down the corridor.

"What *is* that *smell*? Is it *always* so bad?" she started to ask. Then she glanced into an open doorway as they passed, and she did not have to ask. Two busy aides were cleaning up after a half-naked, skin-and-bones woman who had soiled her bed.

One of the aides reached out and closed the door.

Strange sounds came from other doorways as they passed. In one room a wavering voice called, "Nurse . . . nurse . . . nurse . . . nurse . . ." seemingly without end.

A TV blared.

There was a mumble of soft, pain-filled cursing.

"Hello!" called someone behind a toothy grin—was it a man or a woman?—and fluttered a wrinkled hand. "Hello, dearie!"

"Do you want some of this, honey?" An age-bent man bent further over his feeble wife's bed with a dish of ice cream.

From a room at the end of the hall, an aide wheeled out a woman on her way to the shower. There was some kind of a blanket around her—carelessly wrapped, so that her nakedness lay open to the world in spots. Louisa blushed for her and turned to see if Chris had noticed.

His head was still down and his eyes were still shut.

They turned into room 34.

It was a room that belonged in a hospital—hospital beds, two night stands, a closet, curtains to pull around each bed, two stiff, uncomfortable chairs.

There was also part of a bathroom—stool and sink—that they were to share with two women in an adjoining room. Although the door was open, the stool was occupied—by a woman with a soft smile and a drool, who was tied to her throne by a bright green strap.

Wallace closed the door.

3

LOUISA HERSELF

Louisa remembered her first lunch in the dining hall for years: turnips(*overcooked*), green beans (*overcooked*), a small portion of wilty salad (*I hate French dressing*), some instant mashed potatoes (*watery*), and a chunk of very institutional meat loaf, plus a cup of almost-hot tea(*Why in the world do we each have to have our own tea bag? I used to use one three or four times at home!*).

Wallace and Mary left after lunch. It was a tearful parting. Louisa and Chris would have walked them to the door, but, "No, Ma. Better not do it," said Wallace. "They want you to stay in that wheelchair for a while . . . until they get used to what you can and can't do." He smiled half-sadly, and it looked as if he meant the smile for comfort, but it brought no comfort to Louisa's hurting soul—only bitterness.

"And," he went on, "until you get used to being here."

Bitterness churned into rebellion in the hidden places of Louisa's spirit, the ancient jaw clenched with determination, and her nostrils flared. "Wallace Hochstetler," she announced, "Wallace Hochstetler . . . don't you believe it for a minute. I'll *never* get used to being in a place like this." Her eyes shot sparks at him. *"Never!"*

Through the next eight years, Louisa would become aware that there are two principal ways other people handle the anger of the elderly: they turn away and ignore it, or they pat them.

Wallace was a patter. He laid his hand softly on Louisa's shoulder—once, twice, again. "Now, Ma . . ." he said.

Mary turned away. "We've got to go now," she said, pausing at the door. "Come on, Wall." And she was gone—but not quite fast enough. Louisa saw the thing she was not meant to see—the soft, reflected glow of light from the tears on Mary's cheeks.

The deep current of anger within Louisa flared to overwhelming life. She straightened in the wheelchair, extended her arm full length, and pointed a wrathful finger toward the now-vacant doorway. "You!" she said, in a voice that was half croak, half shout. "You, Mary! What are *you* crying for? *You* get to go *home* . . . You get to go home . . . You get to go home."

As she finished, the shout softened to a low moan. She dropped the arm and the accusing finger, and covered her face with her hands, fingers spread. "You get to go home."

Great sobs took Louisa then. She shook her head and began to rock slowly from side to side. And when the sobbing stopped, she whispered softly, "I want to go home, too. I don't want to stay here. I want to go *home!*"

All that Louisa was seemed to flow into the air in those words, and when they were gone from her, she was spent—and sat slumped in her chair waiting for whatever was going to happen to her. There didn't seem to be anything more she could make happen for herself.

A gentle hand reached out then to touch her arm, and for a moment she thought Wallace was still there. But when she looked up, Wallace and Mary were both gone. Chris had struggled out of his wheelchair and come to stand beside her. On his face was written, plain as words, what he was feeling. He dropped to his knees and put his head in her lap, and his arms around her. Louisa touched his head with gentle fingers and held him to her.

For a long time, they both took comfort in that.

The rest of the day passed in a blur, running itself together, scene upon scene, face upon face, word upon word. Louisa and Chris did what they were told, and when nobody told them anything, they sat and did nothing.

At nine o'clock in the evening an aide came and said, "You have to get ready for bed now."

Louisa's eyes darted to the window, where the last sun of evening was still slanting down. "Seems awful early," she said.

"No," said the aide. Not really looking at either of them, she dragged two hospital gowns out of a drawer and plopped one of them on each bed. "It's nine. Time to get into your jammies." She grinned, but her smile wasn't aimed at either of them—just tossed out into the air.

"Dear Lord," thought Louisa. "Jammies?" She looked at Chris, who rolled his eyes toward the ceiling and shrugged his shoulders. "I don't think," he said, "that this is going to be my favorite chapter in life."

For the first time in a very long time, Louisa laughed. It was only a soft chuckle, and it didn't take the edge off the pain of the day. But it did feel good.

The aide helped Louisa into a gown in a surprisingly gentle and kind way—although she never did get around to looking at either of them.

"Night-night," she said, raising the sides on their beds, tucking them in and turning out their light. "Sleep tight."

"And don't," muttered Chris, "let the bedbugs bite." He laughed again, then sighed. "Definitely not my favorite chapter." Almost as soon as the words were spoken, he turned over, and was asleep.

Louisa didn't sleep.

She tried. But there seemed to be things happening in the strange darkness, and those things would not let sleep come close to her.

Once she thought Wallace and Mary had come, and they were going to take her somewhere. But they never stepped out of the shadows, and she remembered finally that they had already come . . . and gone . . . and she had been taken somewhere.

Once she thought that she would like a cup of tea or warm milk to help her sleep. It was then she realized that she would never again be free to get up at night to fix anything for herself.

Once she had to go to the bathroom, but she couldn't seem to get her legs over the side of the bed and get up. She remembered that there was a button to push to call an aide to help her.

When the aide finally came, she was one Louisa had not seen before, and she grumbled, "Well, of course you couldn't get your feet over the side. You're not supposed to. That's why we put these rails up."

She slammed the rail down and pulled Louisa toward the edge. "Maybe later . . . when we're sure you won't fall out. . . ."

"What time is it, please?" Louisa asked humbly as she crawled back under the covers. She didn't feel humble but she didn't want to prompt any more grumbling from the aide, either.

"Ten-thirty," snapped the aide. "Now go to sleep. I hope you don't decide to have me in here every hour or so all night long."

Ten-thirty? It had been a long night already. Snuggling deep beneath the blanket, Louisa's body was lonely for Monroe Street and the old iron bed with its sagging cotton mattress and old, familiar lumps.

So began a habit that was to carry Louisa through many long, lonely nights.

Lying there, relaxed, still, she could not feel the smoothness of the mattress beneath her. Her eyes shut, concentrating on quiet so hard that she scarcely breathed, Louisa could pretend the lumps were there: one under her right shoulder, where she had always wiggled to get away from it before settling down to sleep; a kind of double lump that lay beneath her right foot when she curled up just so; and the soft lump under her pillow, where she had always caressed it with wrinkled fingertips before she finally slept.

On this first night and the many that followed, Louisa begged God to turn her pretending into reality. "Please, God," she would whisper from behind closed eyes.

But when she dared to look again, the bare white walls of the rest home were always there waiting, and the house on Monroe Street was always gone.

On this first night, a flash of lightning made her open her eyes and hope for the sight of faded wallpaper, and a faded picture of Christ knocking at the door.

Though the flashes came again and again, the only answer to her prayer was, "No."

Louisa lay there watching as a tattered cloud wrapped itself around the moon like an aged cloak. Then came more clouds—the crash of thunder—huge drops of rain tapping at her window—and, finally, a downpour.

In spite of the way she felt about the rest home, Louisa found herself most grateful to be sheltered where it was warm and dry. *I'm glad I don't have to be out in all that,* she thought. She settled down with the storm as a companion for the dreams the aged dream at night, and to watch the weary darkness slowly pass.

Toward sunrise, Louisa finally dozed and woke snorting softly, surprised, as she would always be, at where she was.

She woke feeling tired.

It's true then, thought Louisa. *I'm here. I'm really here. And all the good part of my life is over.*

She was to wake every morning for nearly eight years in that same small room—but she never quite got over wanting to go home.

In the summer when cherries were ripe, she wanted to go home to can the fruit.

If she needed a new dress, she wanted to go home and sew.

When she thought about strangers in her house, living there, washing *her* windows, scrubbing *her* floors, she wanted to go home and raise her cracking voice to shout, *Get out, all of you. This is mine!*

She even missed her own bathroom, with the cracks in its porcelain and the toilet that one of the great-grandchildren called "Gramma's embarrassing pot" because it didn't always flush right. But it, too, was home.

The nursing home was not—and never could be. The difference set the tone for Louisa's first days there.

Louisa looked at the shrunken beings around her—people with hair that was thin and brittle, gray and lusterless; people whose skin was wrinkled and dry; people who dared not exert themselves because catching their breath was too much trouble afterwards; people who walked as if they were continually fighting for balance; people who could cut or burn themselves and never know the hurt had happened—and she knew without a mirror that those people were reflections of herself.

Louisa was thinking about that one afternoon when a man wearing an ancient, sagging sweater tottered into the day room. She almost laughed.

"There," she said, clutching Chris's arm. "That's what I'm like, that sweater. I'm old, worn out, and no good to anybody, and there's no hope of ever getting any newer. I never was much for looks, but this whole body has just given up. It sags all over like that sweater."

"Yessir," she said to Chris, to a passing aide and to anybody else who would listen. "I am sure enough like that sweater."

Moments later a young aide strolled by with a cart and a pitcher, offering orange juice.

Louisa had another idea. "I'm like that pitcher, too. Everything in me is being poured out—pretty soon there won't be anything left of me but an outside.

"Yessir," she said again. "I'm like that pitcher, too."

The young aide leaned down close to Louisa's face and poured some juice for her. "Miz B.," he said, confidentially, "You are going to have to make up your mind." He paused, waiting for every mentally competent person within hearing distance to take note of what he was saying. "You are going to have to make up your mind . . . whether you're a *sweater* . . ." He laughed so hard he could barely finish his sentence. "Or a *pitcher*!"

Louisa brushed away the extended hand with the glass of juice and wheeled herself out of the room. "I think," she muttered as she rolled off, "that I am also kind of out of style."

Sometimes they all seemed to be trying awfully hard to make her new again—to get her back in style.

Like the parties, where they wanted her to wear a funny hat and toot on a noisemaker.

Or like the drawing contest.

All the aides were sent scurrying down the halls one morning to empty rooms and bring mobile patients to the day room.

"Come on," they said. "Hurry along now. We're going to have a drawing contest." They shoved Louisa and Chris into the wheelchair line-up and gave them each a tray to write on, a large sheet of paper, and some crayons.

Louisa traced a few trembling lines with the tip of one broken crayon and, stopping, shook her head. "I can't do things like that anymore," she said. "I used to be able to, but I can't now." She dropped paper and crayons on the floor.

They scolded her, of course. An aide came running and picked up the things and said Louisa was a "naughty girl." Whereupon Louisa shoved it all on the floor again.

"I don't want to draw," she said, with all the dignity she could muster beneath the scolding. "I don't *want* to."

The frustrated aide bent again to pick up the scattered items, then tried to get Louisa to take them.

"Oh, for Pete's sake," interrupted a gently commanding female voice behind them, "leave her alone."

And Louisa turned to meet Jessie.

Jessie Henderson was younger than most of the other residents at Parmenter County. Sixty-five, perhaps, and beautiful. Her white hair lay in soft waves around her head. Her features were refined, with eyes sharp, alert, and knowing. Her skin was soft and had, somehow, retained the flush of youth.

Jessie wore an expensive and stylish pantsuit. But because of the kind of person Jessie was, she would have looked well-dressed in an old housecoat or a pair of jeans.

Jessie, too, was in a wheelchair.

"Hello," she said to Louisa, with a wry smile, "Old age is one hell of a way to end a life, isn't it?"

Louisa cringed at the word. "Oh," said Jessie. "You don't like that kind of talk, huh? OK. I won't do it anymore.

"But I don't mind telling you," she went on, "I wish I were dead and could just skip this part of it. As it is, only part of me is dead." She pounded clenched fists on the lower part of her thighs, just above the knees.

A puzzled frown creased Louisa's face.

"Car wreck," said Jessie in reply.

With the words, a curtain seemed to drop between them. In a way, Jessie had left the room. "I loved being alive," she said. Her voice was so soft Louisa could barely hear. "But there's no point to this. I wish," she said again, "that I were dead."

There was something frightening in the woman and her words. Louisa turned and wheeled herself away. There was nothing in the encounter to indicate how close the two of them were to be in the matter of aging—and of dying.

4

HEARTACHES

After the initial contact with Jessie, Louisa had made herself a promise: she would try to adjust. She would try to do better about life in the home. She would stop thinking about herself and see if she couldn't reach out to make life better for some of the people around her.

She meant it, too. But it was so very hard to do. It was hard to stop thinking about herself when there were so many things that bothered her.

Most of the people around her had two major complaints: the food and their children. Louisa had others as well.

Rules at the home were very strict. The routine was stiff, unbending and, at times, uncomfortable.

Hours for getting up in the morning and going to bed at night were set for them as were meal and exercise times.

Only going to the bathroom, thought Louisa. *They still let me decide about that.*

Nights were often boring. She stared into the darkness, wide-awake, thinking about what the daytime had been like.

One of those nights Louisa realized that she needed to make a trip to the bathroom. Well . . . at least it would be something to do.

She rang for a nurse, who did not come. There were so many residents and so few nurses on duty that there were times when it took quite a while to get an answer to a ring. Although Louisa knew the reason for it, she could not help feeling impatient.

She rang again. Nobody came.

Louisa got up by herself. She wasn't supposed to, but she did, shuffling across the floor in the darkness.

Then the nurse came. It was Mrs. Whitehead, on the late shift for a change. "Why, Mrs. B.," she exclaimed. "You aren't supposed to be out of bed alone in the dark."

Like a child, Louisa was scolded all the way to the bathroom and back. By the time the nurse helped her into bed, she felt as if she had been spanked. It was a ridiculous way for a one hundred-year-old woman to be made to feel.

After the first few days, the aides began to grumble about Louisa's long hair. Keeping it neat and clean was a time-consuming chore for them.

"Hey, Mrs. B.," one of them said one morning in the middle of braiding, "how would you like to let me cut your hair?"

Louisa's hands flew to her hair as if to make sure the damage had not already been done. "No!" she cried. "Oh, no!"

The voice of the Apostle Paul tumbled around in Louisa's head. "It is a shame for a woman to be shorn . . . but if a woman have long hair, it is a glory to her," was how Louisa remembered it. In her economy of things, it was a wicked thing—sinful—for a woman to have short hair. She had worn her hair long all of her life; it was part of her faith.

"No!" she said again.

"All right, Mrs. B.," said the aide. "It's all right." But the rest of the braiding, and the winding of the braid into a knot at the back of her head seemed roughly—carelessly—done, and it hurt.

The next time Wallace and Mary came, there were scissors in Mary's purse.

"It has to be done, Mother," she said. "They called me to complain. It takes them so long to do your hair that they have to neglect other people who need them as badly as you do.

"It has to be *done*," Mary said again.

Louisa dropped the hands which she had raised protectively to the braid; her shoulders sank, pulled down by the heavy weight that suddenly sat in her chest.

Mary pulled out hair pins. The scissors rose. And—snip-snip—it was over.

Mary dropped the braid into a waste basket and did some quick trimming just below Louisa's ears. Louisa was left with a thatch of very short, very straight hair, cut straight around.

Heartsick, she started to speak from the ache inside her. "You don't care anything about what *I* want . . . or what I *need*. . . ."

"Mother, I *do* care. I care terribly. It's just that . . ."

"Humph!" Louisa cut her off. Hurting the way she was, she could not listen. All she could do was try to hurt back—to say something that would make them feel as bad as she did—as if that might take some of the sting from her own wounds.

"You'll be glad," Louisa said, softly and deliberately, "when I'm dead. It'll be easier for you."

Mary did not answer. Her head jerked, as though Louisa had reached out and slapped her leaving the stinging, red imprint of an open hand on her face. She hurried from the room without a backward glance. In shocked surprise, Louisa saw that Mary's shoulders were shaking.

I shouldn't have said that, thought Louisa. *Oh, dear God, I should never have said it!*

And Louisa's own wounds felt worse instead of better.

It was several weeks before Mary came back again—when the incident had faded into the past and both of them could pretend they had forgotten it, without really having to say anything about it.

But now, as her daughter disappeared from the frame created by the open door—Mary's left foot and right hand, plus a patch of green pantsuit were the last things Louisa saw—the old woman turned toward her mirror. She was reluctant, almost able to convince herself that it could wait for later—but it couldn't. She had to know how much damage had been done.

The sight of herself, hardly herself at all anymore, was a terrible thing to Louisa. She turned away and covered her eyes with trembling fingers.

"It's too bad," said a voice, "it's too bad that you aren't as invisible to yourself as you are to them. Then you wouldn't have to look at what they've done to you!"

Louisa looked up to see Jessie watching her from a wheelchair half caught in the doorway.

"Invisible?" Louisa said.

"That's how I feel most of the time," Jessie went on. "It's as if they can't see me at all." She backed off in the wheelchair, straightened it, aimed at the door, and entered Louisa's room.

"That's how they treat most of us, you know. Would you care for a cup of tea?" From the side of her chair, Jessie drew a thermos and poured for both of them, while she talked.

"Trouble with us old folks," she said, "is that we aren't attractively packaged. Now if I looked like Garbo or Dietrich or Fonda . . ." she said, and then grinned. "Jane, I mean, not Henry. If I looked like one of them, it wouldn't matter so much that I'm stuck in this damn chair."

Jessie looked up in time to catch Louisa's wince. "Sorry," she said. "I keep forgetting." Her tone became deadly serious. "Please don't be mad. I keep trying to do better. I don't know what I'd do if I didn't have you to talk to. The others"—she waved in a gesture that somehow included the whole building—"The others, most of them, don't know themselves whether they're alive or dead."

She paused and seemed to be waiting for some word of forgiveness. *Well,* thought Louisa, *it sounds as if she needs me. I guess I can put up with a word or two I'm not used to. It is, after all, wonderfully nice to be needed.* A kind of inner sigh of contentment settled down around her soul and brought comfort.

All she said was, "Well . . . "

Jessie leaped upon the word as if it were the one she waited for and went on with her philosophy.

"And so . . . because the package isn't as attractive . . . people kind of skip over us when they look around. They slide their eyes around us and through us, but they never really look *at* us. In a way that makes us invisible."

While Jessie talked, Louisa was looking at her—not around and through, but *at* her, close and hard. The results of the scrutiny surprised Louisa. "Why, Jessie isn't at all like she was when I first met her," she thought.

There was a trace of breakfast on the front of her blouse, and her hair was no longer beauty-shop neat. The lines in her face had been etched more deeply by just a few weeks, and her fingers sometimes danced nervously on the arms of the wheelchair—almost as if making up for toes and legs that could not move at all.

"She's getting older," thought Louisa. "Someday soon she'll be just like the rest of us."

"You know something?" asked Jessie, as she finished the last of her tea. "You know something?" The dark eyes bored into Louisa's soul. "I know what would make me really invisible." She paused for effect, as if hoping Louisa would understand what she meant without her having to say it. "I know. And if I ever figure out a way to do it, I'll do it, too."

With those words, Jessie whirled her chair and was gone.

Louisa was left with a jumble of thoughts, and the memory of something else Jessie had said:

"Any way I could get out of here would be good. Absolutely *any* way. Even taking some pills or something, if I could just get enough of them."

Every Wednesday Wallace wrote to Louisa, and every Thursday the letter arrived. "Dear Ma," it always began. Afterwards, there was always heartache for Louisa, but not because of what the letter said. It was always bright and newsy: "Got my garden in early this year," or "Canned thirty pints of tomatoes," or "Gave a talk at the Christian businessmen's meeting."

But the heartache was in the writing itself. Wallace's hand had begun to shake. His writing trembled on the page. Looking at it, Louisa could see Wallace bent over the lined tablet at the breakfast table, his rough, gnarled fingers holding the pen. And she could see the painstaking, slow determination that moved that pen across the lines to create a letter for her.

It nearly broke her heart.

He's getting old, she thought. *My Wallace. My little boy. He's getting old.* There were days when she wept for him.

There were days, too, when she wept for others.

Minnie Johnson, for example. It was early one morning— Louisa was barely awake—when she first noticed Minnie shuffling up and down the hall, back and forth past Louisa and Chris's door.

Ohhhhh," wailed Minnie as she went. "Ohhhhhh... woe is me!" The sound would increase as she came closer and closer, peak as she appeared in the doorway, then fade as she passed. At the end of the hall, Minnie would turn and start the whole process over again. "Ohhhhhhh!"

Finally Louisa could contain her curiosity no longer. She struggled out of bed and into a robe and went to join the groaning Minnie.

Minnie had already passed, and there was no way that Louisa, impeded by her walker, could catch the other woman, so she waited, partly blocking the hallway, until Minnie came shuffling and wailing back.

Then, "Whatever is the matter?" demanded Louisa.

"Ohhhhhhhh," was the only answer she could get at first.

"What's wrong?" Louisa asked again.

"Ohhhhhh, woe is me!" Minnie had stopped, but she didn't seem to see Louisa. It was as if someone had created a robot and pushed the buttons marked "shuffle" and "wail," but forgot to push the ones marked "see" and "hear," and the eyes and ears were not turned on.

This, thought Louisa, *will never do.*

She reached out and took Minnie by the shoulders, shaking her gently.

"Ohhhhhh!"

Placing her hands at the sides of Minnie's head and forcing her to turn, "Look at me," Louisa said firmly. "Look at me!"

Slowly Minnie's eyes came into focus.

"Now," said Louisa. "What is the matter?"

"They're taking me away from here," moaned Minnie. The tone was the same as before. "I don't know where it is, but they're taking me there. They told me this morning. This is the only home I've got now . . . and they're taking me away."

The eyes began to circle around Louisa again, and emptiness returned to them. Minnie brushed past and was gone, wailing. "Ohhhhhhhh . . .."

There were tears in Louisa's eyes as she went back through the door of room 34.

Although Louisa never really liked room 34, she had tried to turn it into a more pleasant place.

Chris and Louisa had been permitted to bring in a few of their personal things, and the dresser top was filled with pictures. Anyone with twenty-eight great-grandchildren and thirty great-great-grandchildren could fill a dresser top easily enough.

Mary had bought twin spreads covered with a little town colored in soft browns and bright oranges mingled with beige, and the spreads took from the hospital beds some of their institutional look.

Louisa had finally been allowed to have a set of the treasured blue cornflower dishes to set on her nightstand. She almost always ate her meals from them, emptying the food from the institutional plates, bowls, and cups into her own precious ones, where it, somehow, tasted better. After meals, she washed her dishes in the bathroom sink to ready them for the next meal.

In time, their windowsill was filled with potted plants as well as a stuffed animal or two.

"Where did you get that awful purple elephant?" demanded Mary one day when she walked into the room to stare at the collection on the windowsill.

"It was a present," said Louisa, refusing to be shamed by her daughter's opinion of her taste. "I like it."

On a bed or table, there was always a Bible lying open—a large-print edition with a magnifying glass on top—waiting to be read.

While Louisa made her mark on room 34, Parmenter County Nursing Home was making its mark on her.

She got used to the regimentation even though there were times when she was hot and sticky that a Wednesday bath would have been nice instead of a Thursday one.

There were times when a nurse's question—"Let's see, Mrs. B., do you need an enema today?"—made Louisa want to answer, "Do *you?*"

But after a while she learned to keep quiet about those things, and for the most part she adapted.

Eventually, they had to let her out of the wheelchair when she and Chris convinced the authorities that they were able to walk, provided they went at it slowly and carefully. So they made their way, whenever they wanted, through the corridors, Chris gripping the handrail that ran the length of the wall, and Louisa thumping along with her walker. It did not, perhaps, contribute greatly to their self-esteem, but it was a lot better than suffering the indignity of the wheelchairs.

One morning about eleven o'clock, the two of them made their way to the day room. It was time for exercise and singing. The activities director—a tall, severely erect woman who looked as if she should have been somewhere else coaching a basketball team instead of directing a choir of ancients—led both activities.

Dutifully, Chris and Louisa sat in their chairs, swinging their arms and waggling their feet on command.

Then the director turned to song, and one or two quavering voices joined in. It was an incredible thing to watch that woman at work. The way she acted, she might almost have been a cheerleader—except that the cheerleaders Louisa had seen had been a good deal better looking.

"I wish we'd sing a hymn once in a while," Louisa whispered to Chris. They seldom got to church anymore. Nobody came to take them. But hymns would help—even if they did seem out of place with a cheerleader instead of a minister.

They sang some more old favorites—"Down by the Old Mill Stream," and "Put on Your Old Gray Bonnet"—with the director flailing her arms, puffing and grunting while she cheered the vocal ones through their paces and pointed and waved at the silent ones, trying to get them to join in.

There was a comfortable silence when the songs ended. *Let's just sit here a minute, enjoying the quiet,* thought Louisa. *Then we'll go back to our room.*

It was not to be. The cheerleader was off again. "Let's *sing* some more," she said, enthusiastically. "Who has a song you'd like?"

Oh, thought Louisa, *that's nice.* Chris was looking at her as if he expected something fine. She raised her hand, not timidly, but very much aware of all the eyes that would turn her way.

"Could we do 'Lead Kindly Light'?" she asked loudly. It was one of Chris's favorites, and he smiled at her, pleased.

From the reaction of the others, she might almost have set off a firecracker under her chair.

Heads swivelled. Mouths opened. Eyes stared. Two or three people nodded agreement. One woman clapped her hands and said, "Oh, goody."

The activities director's lips twitched with chagrin. "Uh . . . how many of us know that song?" she asked gruffly, as if she were embarrassed by the mention of it.

A scattering of hands were raised—four or five in addition to Louisa's and Chris's. "I'm sorry, honey," said the cheerleader. "I don't think enough of us know that. Who has a *good* song we could sing?"

"Old MacDonald?" asked a tiny, hopeful voice.

"All *right*!" said the activities director, and she was off again. "Old MacDonald had a . . . eee . . . iii . . . eee . . . iii . . . ohhhhhh!"

Things like that were harder to get used to.

Louisa never suggested another song to them. But when the singing was over and she and Chris had hugged the handrails and thumped the walker all the way back to their room, she sat on the bed and sang softly: "Lead, Kindly Light . . .

> . . . amid th'encircling gloom, lead Thou me on!
> The night is dark, and I am far from home;
> lead Thou me on . . .

Chris sat opposite, head down, eyes closed, thumping his fingers on his nightstand in time to her singing.

Something beautiful of the Light touched Louisa's darkness as she sang. She remembered that. Other times, when the darkness pressed, threatening, in about her, she sang again.

Or prayed for visitors to come. Visitors helped so much— like an infusion of life into the atmosphere of decay.

She loved to look up from reading or sleep or daydreaming to see Wallace or Mary or someone else standing in the doorway.

"Hi, Ma!" Wallace would say, crossing the room to put his arm around her and kiss her. "How you doing, Chris?" And he would hold out a hand to shake.

Then he would sit for an hour or two and talk or listen or peel apples—according to what Louisa and Chris wanted.

Sometimes the visitors brought children, and that was better yet. The brittle people, muddled in their minds, who so often surrounded Louisa—although they were living and breathing—still spoke of death and endings. Children spoke of life and beginnings.

It was after a child had been there one day that Louisa finally realized what she should be doing to make the rest of life worthwhile.

It was the contrast that did it, probably, more than anything.

The child—a bouncy and exuberant little boy, full of love and excitement and energy—hugged his unknowing grandfather and departed, laughing. As he went, Louisa turned to Chris.

What she saw was a contrasting age and weariness— nothing of bounce or laughter left.

I love you, Chris Basinger, she thought then. *I love you . . . and I'm going to forget my own heartaches and see if I can't help you bear some of yours for a while."*

She reached for his hand and held it.

5

EARLY MEMORIES

The early days and weeks in the nursing home passed quietly for Louisa. As they drifted by, she decided that two things were very important: remembering from day to day who she was and who she had been. She often tried to do this in the lonely hours of the night, while Chris and the others slept.

Lying there in bed, she sometimes could not tell whether her dreams came while she was awake or while she slept. She allowed herself to drift back in time, sometimes into her own memories, sometimes beyond, to things she knew only because people who loved her had told her stories.

On the night of her birth nearly a century before, an icy March wind had been whistling down the chimney and through the stove pipe to rattle the windows from inside as well as out. The high-ceilinged room was drafty, and it was cold anywhere more than a couple of feet from the stove. Yet the man deliberately turned from the warmth to find a chair in the farthest corner, where he sat down, stood up, paced four steps to stare out the window into snow-swirling darkness, wrung his hands, paced four steps back, and sat again.

Sweat beaded his forehead and his upper lip, and the blue linen shirt had dark circles under the arms. Every sound from the bedroom seemed to increase the amount of moisture he had to contend with, and he raised an arm frequently to run the back of his sleeve across his face.

"Dear God," he pled, listening to the soft, frightened cries from the other room. Most of the cries were soft. She was a brave woman, after all, and she only screamed once. Or was it twice? Perhaps twice as the agony grew more than she could bear, and sound was torn from her throat in some strange way so that she heard it from far away, as if some other woman had screamed.

"Dear God, why must it be this way? Is it always so?" It was one of the few times in his life he prayed. Henry Nussbaum was never much for prayer—not until much later in his life, when, just weeks before he died, he learned to know God. But now he was suffering, and so—despite his usual disinclination—he prayed.

His suffering lasted for just over nineteen hours. The sun had risen behind clouds and dragged itself slowly past noon. Shortly after the second scream, he heard the wailing of his newborn child, and a neighbor woman appeared, smiling, in the bedroom door.

"Mr. Nussbaum?" The eyes he turned toward her were a little frightened as well as a little hopeful. "It's over." She beckoned to him, stepping aside for him to enter the room.

At the foot of the bed, leaning slightly forward over the wooden bedstead he had made himself, he stopped. His wife was pale, and she looked tired. Her eyes seemed hot and bright as she watched his entrance.

But a soft smile was on her lips. She whispered, "Look," as she reached to uncover a tiny, perfect girl baby. "See what God has given us, Henry?"

There was a sadness in his voice, remembering her pain, as he answered, "In sorrow thou shalt bring forth children . . . ."

Her smile only deepened. They had both been raised in religious homes. She could quote scripture as well as he. "But afterwards," she said, "after the bringing forth, the father and mother shall be glad, and she that bear shall rejoice."

"It's a girl," he said when she covered the child again. "We'll name her Louisa—after your mother."

That, he knew, would please her. She closed her eyes, almost asleep.

But it did not please him—not enough, anyhow. His face and shirt were still damp with the sweat that had broken out while he listened to her cries. He had to say something else, more to comfort himself, perhaps, than to affect her.

And so he made the promises—about how faithfully and how well he would care for the two of them.

By the time he finished, the mother and the new child were both asleep.

Well, he thought, wondering if he had been insulted. *"Well!"* Taking a blanket, he slipped back out to the other room and the couch, where he too fell asleep, snoring softly through his young man's beard.

He was newly come from Switzerland, where he had herded cattle on the hills for his father. Swiss, a dialect of German, was the language of his home, as well as of most of his Mennonite neighbors at Bluffton.

A custom butcher by trade, years later, he would have his own butcher shop. But in the early days of his move to America and his marriage he drove a butcher wagon from farm to farm, wherever he was needed. All his equipment was on that wagon. When someone wanted to butcher a pig or a steer, they would send for Henry.

It was a good living. And it was good to sleep, confident that he could take care of little Louisa and her mother—as well as others who would follow.

He could have, thought Louisa, stirring softly beneath her covers a hundred years later. *He could have . . . but he didn't always.*

Six more children were added to the family. When the birthing was finished, Louisa had three brothers, Fred, William, and Henry and three sisters, Bertha, Emma, and Sarah.

With each new arrival Papa found the cries easier to bear. His gratitude for the safety of his wife and baby became less each time as the promises were harder to make. And each time, sleep came more easily to him.

Like most children, a young Louisa had loved to draw. She had a slate and some chalk that had belonged to a cousin, and she drew trees, houses, flowers, mothers, fathers, rabbits, horses, and cows. But her favorite things to draw were cats—

funny round creatures with pointed ears and drooping whiskers, long tails and belly buttons—that somehow never quite
looked like cats, and always had to be explained.

Without an explanation, someone was sure to say, "My, oh
my, Louisa, that certainly is a nice mouse!" or "Well, I don't
think I ever saw a rabbit with a long tail before."

But if she remembered to explain, they always said, "You
sure draw fine cats, Louisa!"

Her drawing always was a pleasure to her—until the day
she found a pencil and decided to draw something more per-
manent. The beginnings of it were on the scraps of paper she
had found around the house and barn. But those had been pre-
viously used by others and were not wholly satisfactory. Then
she remembered where she had seen beautiful, white, *empty*
sheets of paper. Running, she found them again, and used her
pencil to fill them with cats.

Finished, Louisa sighed the deep sigh of a contented soul
and put the paper away. Every so often, afterwards, she would
take it out again and run her finger over the cats—or add
another in some tiny, empty space she had overlooked.

But when her father discovered her wonderful pages of
cats in the front and back of the family Bible, he gave Louisa a
whipping like she had never had before. Dragging her outside,
he held her against the peach tree with one hand as he broke off
a switch with the other. While Louisa danced and howled, he
laced the backs and sides of her bare legs with welts. After that
she had lost much of her interest in drawing.

There had been plenty of other things to keep a child busy
all those years ago, when Papa had driven his butcher wagon all
around Bluffton and had kept all the promises he had made to
his wife and children at birthing times.

There had been school and her friends, Elizabeth and Carrie. There had even been that mean Will'am.

Will'am always wanted to be best in everything: spelling,
arithmetic, geography, even skipping rope. When the girls
started, "How many kisses did she get . . . 1 . . . 2 . . . 3 . . . 4 . . ."
outside at recess, Will'am would always come along and boast
that he could jump rope better than any old girl. He never did

anything to prove it, but he was awfully good at the bragging part.

Inside the school room, though, it was a different story. Will'am was really good at his studies.

He knew how to spell almost everything, and if little Louisa Nussbaum missed a word, he would taunt her unmercifully. "That ain't how you spell it, silly," he would singsong. "You're not so good in spelling, are you?"

And if she couldn't remember whether Columbus or Cincinnati was the capital of Ohio, Will'am would whisper for her ears alone, "Try Mansfield, silly. Or maybe it's Bucyrus. Or *Pandora!*" The idea of the last would make him lean his head over the rough plank desk shaking with laughter.

When Louisa was about eight, the family moved to the tiny country village of Pandora, some five miles distant, where so many of the people were smiling, friendly Mennonites, the streets were dusty beneath the hot summer sun, and there was a covered bridge over Riley Creek.

Moving to Pandora wasn't so bad. It was moving away from Bluffton that was hard. The teacher at the school and the other children had a picnic the day she left—a farewell party. She kept looking at them and thinking, "I wonder if I'll ever see Samuel again . . . or that mean Will'am . . . or Carrie . . . or . . . ."

Her father came in the big wagon with their household goods and picked her up at the school, and they drove away to Pandora. When Louisa looked back, she saw her best friend, Elizabeth, scuffing slowly through the dust as if drawn by the wagon moving down the road.

Young Louisa thought there were tears on Elizabeth's cheeks. She knew there were streams of them on her own.

While Louisa grew to love Pandora and its people, and she was to spend most of her life there, the pain of that move was remembered.

"Good-by, Elizabeth," said the aging Louisa to herself the night she dreamed about the move from Bluffton. "Good-by." And she turned back to her unfriendly mattress at Parmenter

County Nursing Home and to the job of making do with what life had given her for an ending.

In spite of Will'am, young Louisa had liked school most of the time. On other nights, old Louisa remembered that she had learned to like school in Pandora as well. But she had missed a lot of it during those years, because every so often, she needed to stay out for a while and work for nearby families. Often she had to go back and catch up before she could go on.

When she finally finished the sixth grade, her schooling was over. After that, she spent most of her time working in other people's homes.

When Louisa was sixteen, she went to work for the Dave Diller family. Her pay was a dollar per week, plus room and board. After three years with the Dillers, there were other families, and her wages rose to a dollar and fifty cents per week. The raises in pay seemed like a tremendous thing at the time—almost enough to take her breath away with excitement. But then, in those days calico and cotton dress goods cost from 15 to 40 cents a yard, so the increase represented considerable investment in new clothes alone, if she had chosen to spend it in that way.

Part of the reason for her working was that Louisa's papa developed a habit of disappearing. After the family moved to Pandora, her papa remembered all his promises about taking care of his wife and children, and he kept them at first.

But promises that seem economically and physically easy to keep may be something harder for the soul of a man.

Over the next few years Papa began taking a little time off from his family now and again. Periodically, he would leave the town without a butcher and his wife and children without support.

The first time it happened, Mama went nearly wild with fear for him before she discovered what was wrong. Papa waved good-by one morning and went off down the road in his wagon, leaving them to assume that he had work for the day.

At supper time that evening Mama set the table for all of them, but delayed the meal, expecting at any moment to hear the plunk of tired hoofs down the road and Papa coming in to join them.

He never came. After a while, she fed the littlest children and put them to bed. Then she fed the older ones and sent them off. Finally she cleared the table, leaving a covered plate for Papa on the back of the stove.

Louisa, shaken, lay awake a long time, listening to the rattle of dishes being washed and stored, then to the gentle squeak of the rocker while Mama waited up for him. Louisa could hear her voice now and again, praying. "Dear God . . . oh, Father God . . . Father . . . Father . . . please, Jesus."

In the morning the covered plate was still there, the stew dried out, gummy, and stuck, to the dish, making it hard to wash.

Mama struggled up from the rocker where she had spent the night, to herd them off to school.

It was three days before they had word about Papa—and that was just by accident. At least, in those days, Louisa had thought it was an accident. Later, when her faith was more mature, she wondered if Mama's God hadn't made it happen that way in answer to prayer.

The next door neighbor woman came over to tell Mama, "Say . . . my man saw yours over Findlay way yesterday. What's he doin' over there? Got a big job of work lined up?"

And so Mama knew.

Because she didn't know when he would be back—or *if* he would be back—and because she had no way to care for the children, she sent them to local farmers to work for room and board.

Louisa missed her family terribly in those days. The first night away from home, she discovered that if she lay on her back, hands behind her head, elbows jutting outward toward the edge of the bed, and cried, she got tears in her ears.

She repeated this experiment more times than she ever wanted to remember. And she made a vow that, years later, she would be called on to keep: "God in heaven, as you are my witness. Never will I turn children of mine out of my house for any reason. I would rather be hungry at home with Mama and the children than lie here in somebody else's bed with a full stomach and cry myself to sleep."

Louisa was nineteen years old when Amos came striding down a church aisle and into her life. He was one of the Bluffton Hochstetlers, come to visit Pandora relatives.

He wasn't particularly handsome. As a matter of fact, he was skinny as a fence rail, and tall, like the rest of his family. Folks made jokes about the "tall, skinny Hochstetlers," any one of whom was said to be able to outwork a team of six mules. The only problem, said one farmer, was that a Hochstetler could also out-eat the mules, so it was generally cheaper in the long run just to work the mules.

There was a gentle ruggedness about young Hochstetler that immediately attracted Louisa's attention.

Her first sight of him was from the back when he came to church on Sunday with his Pandora relations. They were late and came marching down the aisle past Louisa, right in the middle of the second verse or so of the first song. She could see an embarrassed red crawling up Amos's neck and ears.

Finding his seat a couple of rows ahead of her, he joined in the singing so lustily that she spent much of the service admiring the rich, earnest voice that lifted such a volume of praise to the Lord.

After the sermon, the Pandora relatives of young Hochstetler were among the church-goers who were invited home for Sunday dinner at the Nussbaum's. And, of course, they brought Amos along.

By the end of that afternoon, Louisa felt she knew him well.

Amos was the proud descendant of Jacob Hofstedler, an Amishman who had arrived in Philadelphia on September 1, 1736. He had fled from Switzerland, where the Amish and the Mennonites were severely persecuted.

Since Jacob was unable to write, his name was always written by others when it had to be recorded. These others came as close to his pronunciation as they could, but in the records of the time—captain's list, land entries, and the like—the name was variously recorded as *Hoofstetler, Hooshstedler, Hostedler, Hostetter, Hoffstetler, Hostetler,* and *Houghstadler.*

By the time members of the family learned to read and write, most of Amos's relatives had settled on Hochstetler as the preferred form.

Amos told her this family history that first day with laughter and pride.

He told her other things which left no room for laughter—only for sorrow. With a look in his eyes that said he longed for such heroic days, Amos told of ancestors who had died or been captured by Indians because they would not lift a hand—or a gun—against another human being.

"The Amish, you know," he said to his new Mennonite friend, "well, they aren't just people who dress funny and use hooks and eyes instead of buttons."

"I mean, they're Christians first. And they really *believe* in their God."

Was there something Louisa should have noticed then? Amos had said *"their* God," instead of *"our* God"—or just "God." If she should have perceived a hidden message, she did not, and Amos continued.

"They are ready to show their faith by a life of obedience, even though that obedience involves hardship and loss of all that people hold dear."

"I know," said Louisa, looking around her at the men in their plain, black suits and the simple, dark dresses of the women. She and her family and friends were not so far from that. "I understand."

Amos grinned. "I guess you do."

The grin gave way to a frown. "But a lot of people don't."

Then he told the story of what had happened to Jacob—and how Jacob had proved his obedience to God.

"He was my great-grandpa, back a ways," said Amos. "I guess he could have saved a lot of lives and saved himself a lot of trouble if he would have shot a few Indians—but he refused.

"It was September 19, 1757. Jacob and his family were in bed asleep when all of a sudden the dog started carrying on.

"One of Jacob's sons went to the door and opened it, and somebody shot him in the leg.

"They knew right away it was Indians. He barely got the door shut in time to keep the attackers out.

"Then when they looked out the window, they could see the Indians standing a ways off like they were making plans.

"It wasn't that the family didn't have any guns. They kept guns and ammunition for hunting and such.

"Two of the sons, Joseph and Christian, got ready to shoot. They figured they could kill a couple of the Indians and drive the rest off. But my granddaddy held as close to the doctrine of nonresistance as any man I've ever heard of, and he wouldn't let them use the guns.

"The Indians set fire to the house, and the family went down into the cellar. When the fire started breaking through the floor, they splashed cider on the flames to put them out.

"When morning came, they saw most of the Indians had gone, and it was getting so hot in the cellar they could hardly stand it anymore. So they climbed out through a window.

"But there was this one young warrior—name of Tom Lions, about eighteen years old—he had stayed behind to pick up some ripe peaches from Jacob's trees. When he saw them escaping, he called the others back.

"My granddaddy stood there, praying and weeping and holding onto his God, while he watched the Indians massacre part of his family and lead the rest off, captive."

There was sadness in Amos's eyes, but a glow, too. Louisa read that glow as zeal for what he believed and a promise of his own faithfulness and obedience to God. If she had been told then that she was wrong, she would not have believed it.

Louisa's own soul was stirred, as if the same glow in her had been lit by Amos. And already, something within her began to whisper, *I could love you, Amos Hochstetler. I could love you.*

A year later, they were married.

6

AMOS

Visitors at the nursing home sometimes triggered Louisa's memories. When a particularly handsome young man and his wife of a few months visited the day room one weekend, Louisa thought about the early days of her marriage to Amos. Sometimes they were painful memories.

She and Amos had made their first home in a one-room log house, south of Pandora in Allen County. Louisa could remember that house as clearly as if she had walked through it only yesterday.

The logs were rough, splintered, and gray. There were no doors or windows; that is, there were openings where doors and windows might have been, but nothing to fill the openings except the carpet that they had hung in place.

They were happy in that house, as happy as Louisa could ever remember being at any time in her life.

Amos hired out to do farm work. Louisa pumped water for a big herd of cattle to pay the rent. She kept the house as neat and tidy as a log house with a puncheon floor could possibly be. All of her life Louisa was a good housekeeper.

Their cooking was done on an old wood stove that served to heat the cabin as well. Louisa never minded. As a matter of fact, she loved that stove. It was always nice and warm, and she could keep food hot on it for her new husband if he was late.

Their first child was conceived beneath a Dutch windmill quilt, on a rope bed with a straw tick, and the fresh, sweet smell of the new tick made Louisa think of nothing so much as a tumble in the hay.

She never admitted that thought to anyone. She had blushed thinking it, even though she was well and securely married. But she thought it, nonetheless.

They lived in that house through the summer until Louisa realized there was a baby on the way. Then Amos found what he thought was a better place for them. It was another log house, in the country near Beaverdam a few miles away, but with windows and doors.

But it also had rats. The muffled sound of gnawing beneath the floor woke them in the middle of their first night there.

Louisa awoke slowly—drifting in and out of sleep—when the chomping teeth and the scrabbling feet forced their way into her pleasant dreams and turned them into nightmares.

"Amos!" she had shouted into the darkness, reaching toward his side of the bed to pat him awake with a hand on his shoulder. "What *is* it?"

She had answered her own question before he woke enough to talk. Except for the sleep and the dream, she never would have been afraid at all.

"Rats," she said. And rats they were.

Amos rolled over and went back to sleep. Louisa rearranged the bulk of her pregnant body, searching for a comfortable spot on the straw tick, only to lie awake for hours listening to the scrabble and the gnaw before she finally was able to sleep.

Yet in spite of their near poverty, and in spite of the long-tailed rodent neighbors who moved right in with them, it was a good life.

They worked hard, but there was love and laughter and great joy for Louisa in those days.

There were times when she could hardly bear to look at Amos because that look always brought an overwhelming sense of love for him and for the child she carried. She forced herself not to look, so that she could get on with the business of living.

It was after the baby was born that she first discovered that her tall, slender husband had faults. He wouldn't go to church with her anymore, and he gave up pretending to believe what he did not really believe. Amos liked to stay away from home late at night once in a while—a thing she could not understand, because she hated being away from him. And his temper flared unreasonably at times, leaving her hurt and feeling unloved.

At those times she would think to herself, *I would never have spoken so to him.*

Their first son, Wallace, was born in the second log house. After that Amos built them a four-room frame house just three miles down the road from Pandora and just across the county line into Allen County.

The house had plank floors, with no rugs—but no rats, either—and it seemed very fine. In those days, more than half the farm homes around Pandora were just crude log houses. A frame house, by comparison, bordered on luxury.

One of Louisa's great delights in those days was to walk to Pandora to visit her parents. Every so often she would put the baby in his buggy and start off down the road for town. She always put several loaves of homemade bread in the lower part of the buggy to contribute to meals.

"I must have looked pretty funny," she would say, years later, telling about the walks, "walking along with a buggy full of bread and a baby."

Louisa was pregnant again, and soon enough there was no walking anywhere.

Jacob and Mary were both born, in rapid succession, in the frame house.

Not long after their births, Amos moved his family to Lima, the county seat, where he began work for the Pennsylvania Railroad as a freighthouse foreman.

Life, though, with Amos was not at all what Louisa had expected it to be. She had married a small-town boy, the proud descendant of Amish ancestors. She had married a man devoted to his wife, his family, and, she thought, to his God.

Six years later she found herself married to a man who was more interested in making a place for himself in the world than he was in his wife, his children, or his God.

It was frustrating . . . and it hurt. Dear Lord Jesus, how it had hurt! There were nights when she lay in bed alone and wept and prayed for him—wherever he was—until he came away from his cronies at last to crawl in bed beside her.

Yet she loved him. And she knew her duty to God and husband. Faithfully she kept his house, fed and cared for his children, provided for his needs, and warmed his bed.

The last of their children, Oliver, was born following their move to Lima. It was after Oliver's birth that the real trouble began. Almost as if he had taken lessons from Papa, Amos began to leave his family to fend for themselves more and more.

Oh, dear Jesus, thought Louisa. *It was hard in those days. It was so hard.*

Harder than life in a nursing home? She wondered. How would a person determine a thing like that? Those days, when she lived through them, had seemed as if they were about as hard as life could get. But in the home it seemed different. At least she was young then, fit to struggle with the hardness, able to take her life in her own hands and come to the unspeakable decision that had caused whispers everywhere she went, for a long time afterward.

There came at last, perhaps inevitably, a night when Amos did not come home at all. All night long Louisa slept alone in the huge double bed. It had seemed small enough with two in it, but it was far too big for one person. Her hand kept reaching out for him in the darkness, patting the covers to see if he had slipped under them unnoticed, hoping he was home. In the morning she could see by first light that what the patting hand had told her in the darkness was true.

For an instant Louisa could hear again the squeak of the rocker and her mother's prayer—"Dear God . . . oh, Father God . . . please, Jesus"—on the first night that her Papa had not come home.

Louisa rolled over and pressed her face into the pillow. "Oh, Mama . . . ," she whispered to the striped ticking. "Oh, Mama . . . poor, darling Mama. I understand at last."

Amos appeared later in the day, his face swollen and his hair mussed. His clothes were rumpled, and he seemed embarrassed to have the children see him slipping in.

Beyond that, he did not appear to know whether he should be sheepish or belligerent. But he said he was sorry, and he asked her to forgive him.

She did. It had not yet occurred to Louisa that there was anything else to do. "Unto seventy times seven," said the Word. She could forgive at least that often.

As a matter of fact, she never kept track of his account. In case he went over 490 offenses, she intended to keep right on forgiving. After all, God had forgiven her much.

That was her intent.

His disappearances, though, became longer and more frequent. He brought a smaller portion of his money home to the family each payday. At last the night came when she had to send the children to bed with no supper—because there was no food in the house.

On that night Louisa paced the floor in her kitchen and spoke aloud to the walls all the things she would like to have said to her husband.

"Amos, your children went to bed hungry."

"Amos, you are not much of a husband anymore."

"Amos, you are nothing at all as a father anymore."

"Amos . . . how *could* you do this to us?"

"Amos . . . ."

"Amos . . . I love you . . . ."

And on that night Louisa knelt, broken, beside one of her kitchen chairs and poured out her soul to God with an offering of bitter salt tears.

For herself Louisa might never have thought of the other. The idea was too much a stranger to her way of life for her to consider it as a way to help herself.

It was, at last, the hunger of her children that brought the thought to her mind: *I could leave him.*

Even to entertain the idea made Louisa feel as if she had pronounced a curse on herself.

Such a thing could never be. Divorce for a Mennonite, a member of the Egli Church was unspeakable . . . unthinkable, even. Her whole world would be destroyed.

Yet Louisa *had* thought of it, and she stood shamed and humiliated before herself and her God. For a long time, no one else knew.

Something has to be done! she scolded herself. *You can't go on like this.*

Even when there was food in the house, often Louisa did not join the children for supper.

"Aren't you going to eat, Ma?" Wallace would ask, looking worried as he said it.

"No, son. I already had a little something," Louisa would reply, lying to ease his pain. "I'm not really hungry. You children go ahead and eat."

It didn't bother her all that much. She thought of the hunger as an offering to God on behalf of her children, and she praised God because on those nights they, at least, had food in their stomachs before they climbed the stairs to bed.

Then came an evening when it bothered her terribly. Turning unexpectedly from the stove when Wallace didn't know she was looking, she saw him break his own portion of bread into three pieces. Sliding the pieces onto the younger children's plates, he held a finger to his lips and mouthed the words, "Don't tell Ma!" before she caught his eye. He started guiltily and shoved a spoon into the watery bean soup in his bowl.

She didn't make him take the bread back. He was his mother's son, after all. A gift like that had to be honored.

When he passed her chair later on his way upstairs, Louisa reached out to touch his sleeve as he brushed past. Wallace paused to look down at her, expecting to be scolded.

She said nothing. She held his eyes and his sleeve for a moment, then offered a firm nod of approval, with a smile that almost got away from her and turned to tears.

If I left him now, she thought, *if I left Amos, maybe there wouldn't have to be a divorce.* Louisa shuddered when the word ran through her mind, as if it left dirty footprints behind.

Maybe I could just go and take the children home to Pandora and make a life for them there, among friends. I could tell people that he left me; it's almost true."

Again she fell to her knees by that kitchen chair.

"My God . . . my very dear Lord . . . my Beloved, what am I to do?"

Anger engulfed Louisa then—anger at Amos, at the children, at herself, even at God.

"Amos . . . ." She tried, as she had done on other nights, to imagine a conversation with him in which she could pour out all of her worry and anger.

"Amos . . . ." But this night she could not begin the conversation.

And this night, there was no "Amos . . . I love you" to end it. She had been hurt too badly. There was too much anger in her soul.

In that anger, Louisa turned again to God, and she spoke out to him things that she might never otherwise have said— even to herself.

"I don't understand you!" she raged, as she knelt with her face pillowed on her arms against the chair, angry tears dripping onto the wood. "I don't understand why you are letting this happen to us!

"He was such a good man! I thought he would live a godly life and lead me and the children deep into the best things you have for us.

"And instead . . . *this!*"

"You should *never* . . . ." Louisa raised her voice and her face heavenward. There was fierce, brief anger in both. " . . . You should never have made me a mother if you meant for me to sit by and watch my children go hungry!"

For a long moment Louisa stopped, appalled by her own audacity. Her breath refused to come, except in short, quick gasps, like a child who fights to stop crying. But she whispered the word again into the darkness, more firmly than before: *"Never!"*

As suddenly as it had come, Louisa's anger was gone. Her tears became tears of repentance, and she dropped her head, sobbing. "Oh, dear God, I am so *sorry!* I didn't mean to talk to *you* that way. What are we to do?"

The storm was over. She felt herself forgiven.

Yet of that stormy night, one single fact remained: Louisa could not be the kind of mother who sat and watched her children go to bed hungry.

It was some time before she did anything about it. There was still great confusion in her mind. All of her family background, her religious and moral training, her faith, cried out "No!"

Only her knowing heart, with help from the logical side of her mind, said, "Yes—it will have to be so."

For that time, Louisa waited, her heart losing the battle.

Then came the prying neighbor who announced over strawberry tea, "Louisa, I could have sworn I saw your Amos last night with . . . but, of course, it couldn't have been."

Louisa knew, too, that it couldn't have been. He had been guilty of desertion, and the mental cruelty that left her aching because of her children's pain, but adultery? No. Never. Not Amos.

She knew it, and she knew it firmly—right up until the night she was out helping Nona Hanson with her baby.

Over the years Louisa had gained a certain amount of practical knowledge about midwifery and nursing, although she had no formal training, just contact with other women. Now it was not at all unusual for her to be called out to help friends with childbirth or illness.

She had been out very late that night, and she was tired. The baby had been trying for twenty hours or more to make his way into the world. It was just after midnight when he finally succeeded.

Louisa left mother and child in the care of a maiden aunt and started for home. Wallace was with her. He was only fourteen, but he didn't like her to walk alone at night. That part of town could be rough sometimes.

Louisa and Wallace were walking, both silent, through a misting rain when they saw the man and woman. He had his arm around her, and she was looking up at him, laughing.

Wallace immediately stepped in front of his mother and turned to put his hands on her shoulders, as though to block her view.

Louisa took his hands, gently lowered them to his sides, and stepped around him.

She watched as the man and woman turned up the steps of a battered house. He stopped to kiss her on the porch before they went in.

Numbness crept over Louisa's mind and body. It was of a piece with the exhaustion she had carried away from the birthing. It almost overwhelmed her.

For a moment Louisa felt almost as if she were floating, no longer in touch with the damp ground beneath her.

When she lifted her eyes to Wallace's face, she saw the tears mingling with the rain on his cheeks before his head dropped.

"It's not him, Ma," he mumbled. "It's somebody who looks like him." Traces of panic filtered through his voice. "Papa wouldn't do a thing like that, Ma. He wouldn't!"

Louisa squared her shoulders, willed strength into her legs—and into Wallace too—and went home.

"We will not," she said to Wallace, "speak of this—ever. Not to anybody."

All that night Louisa lay awake with a great, sinking emptiness where her heart should have been.

She kept seeing Amos.

She saw him walking down the aisle at church, the first time she met him.

She saw him at their wedding. She heard the minister saying, "Until death . . ." and she felt herself knowing that their marriage was forever.

She felt him lift her to carry her through the doorway of that first log cabin, past the hanging carpet and the rough-hewn table to the straw tick. Her head was on his shoulder, and his face was gentle and loving above her.

She saw him bending over the bed on the night Wallace was born, his face filled with awe. And she saw him reaching just one finger to touch the soft fuzz on the baby's head.

She saw him walking home from work nights—first from a neighboring farm, then from the freighthouse—sitting down to supper with them, smiling, glad to see them, happy for the end of his day, and pleased to be home.

Then, because she could not help it, she saw the empty bed beside her and the strange woman who had walked down the street with a tall, slim man and raised her face to kiss him before she took him into her house.

Louisa cried that night—more than she had at any other time in her life. More tears would come later, but first there were things that had to be done.

So it was that Louisa became a pioneer in an area she would never have chosen for herself. In a time and among a devout people where divorce was considered a shameful thing and a disgrace, she sought a divorce.

And it had been hard for her.

When Louisa saw a lawyer, she had to talk about the incident that she had told Wallace never to mention. She had to tell him that her husband was gone, and that she had seen him with another woman, that her table and her bed were empty, and that her children were hungry.

The telling seemed to cheapen her. It was as if she were emptied of everything of value: self-esteem, will power, even love. She could not escape the nagging voice at the back of her mind that whispered over and over, *For shame! For shame!*

Her words seemed to hang, condemning her, in the air of the lawyer's office. And as if her own opinion were not enough, a look came in the lawyer's eyes and a twist to his lips that indicated his opinion of this loose woman who sat before him.

Louisa knew that thought was in his mind. She tried to pretend that she didn't, but something in her sank lower and lower under his condemnation.

His words were nice enough—polite, professional. Yet beneath that veneer the contempt for a woman who could sink to Louisa's depths was evident.

Louisa's mind was made up, and it was not to be changed. She was not a woman tossed to and fro, carried about by every wind. Once she had made up her mind to a thing, she stuck with it. She did not change easily.

So, in spite of the implications that seemed to permeate the air of the lawyer's office, Louisa went ahead with her plans.

She wavered only once. That was the morning she came yawning down the stairs to find a letter from Wallace propped on the breakfast table.

"Dear Ma," it began, and it ended, "Please don't do it. *Please,* Ma. I love you, Wallace."

Louisa's determination trembled.

Still she believed that she was doing what was right, and this rightness bolstered her courage. Despite Wallace's plea, she went on with plans to divorce Amos.

"The Bible only allows one reason for divorce," she told him later, in answer to his letter. "I am a Bible-believing woman, Wallace Hochstetler. And don't you forget it. Your father has given me both heart-reason and Bible reason for divorce, and we are going to be free. The church may or may not understand, but that's not up to me."

Louisa was thirty-four years old when she stood with her four children in the county courthouse to see the judge nod his head and hand her the paper that said she no longer had a husband.

On the other side of the room Amos dropped his head into his hands and wept. Louisa could not look at him. She did not dare.

Oliver, who was then six years old, went to live with his father. It was part of the agreement. His leaving broke Louisa's heart into even smaller pieces, but at least she knew he would not go to bed hungry.

Wallace, fourteen; Jacob, thirteen, and Mary, eleven, stayed with their mother.

They saw little of Amos after that. He did not contribute to their continuing support because some property was sold and divided at the time of the divorce.

There was no reason to see him again. Louisa didn't think she wanted to—but sometimes she dreamed she was looking for Amos and couldn't find him. Or she dreamed he had died, and she went to his funeral and wept.

After the divorce hearing was over, Louisa took the three older children back to Pandora where she found a job, sewing, in a small overall factory. It was hard work, ten hours a day, and it was not enough. The children also had to work at odd jobs.

Wallace worked in a barbershop, sweeping up and cleaning spittoons until he was fifteen. Then he got a job at Noah Schumacker's store, selling shoes.

Jacob worked at the overall factory.

Mary did odds and ends of housework for neighbors who gave her pennies plus an occasional peppermint stick or a pat on the head.

Louisa added to her knowledge about practical nursing until after a while she was able to quit the factory. For fifteen years she supported her family by bringing babies into the world and helping the old leave it with as much dignity and comfort as possible.

She was wrong about one thing, though. Her idea that it would be an obvious and a simple thing to take the children back to Pandora and make a life there among friends was wrong.

When they learned about the divorce, friends were suddenly not as friendly.

Some of the worst of the criticism came from members of the church. Louisa and her family were shunned.

Other women crossed the street to avoid speaking. Children turned and ran.

In the early days of their return to the little town, Louisa's children were sometimes hungry. Outside hanging up wash one afternoon, she saw a neighbor in the garden next door throwing away extra produce. The woman turned and looked away, pretending not to see Louisa. She was a divorced woman. Her children were touched and contaminated by her sin.

Mothers told their young not to play with Mary.

Wallace had a girlfriend who had to quit seeing him when her parents found out that his parents were divorced.

And every so often Jacob came home from school with his shirt torn and his nose bleeding, because one of the other children had said something about his mother or sister. Under such pressure, he soon lost the traditional pacifist beliefs of his Mennonite ancestors.

It was a long time before people could accept the children for themselves instead of ostracizing them for what their parents had done. It was even longer before the children were able to accept the fact of the divorce. Wallace, for one, always spoke of it as a tragedy—when he could bring himself to speak of it at all.

It was much longer before people could accept Louisa.

And it certainly seemed that what they thought was most ugly. It seemed that Louisa herself was about the only one who thought she might have been right.

Most of the Swiss background Mennonites in the Bluffton-Pandora area were part of the General Conference Mennonite Church. Louisa's family, however, belonged to the "Defenseless Mennonites," a small group begun after the Civil War by an Amishman, Henry Egli, who lived near Berne, Indiana. Egli had charged that the Mennonite faith was becoming indifferent to spiritual matters. The "Egli Amish" stressed personal conversion, living peaceably with all, and a strict life of personal piety. Divorce was unthinkable.

The two local ministers of her congregation, Elder Kreutzer and Elder Specht, made that point abundantly clear. They had come to visit Louisa not long after the divorce to register their disapproval and that of the church.

Louisa had heard them outside the door before they knocked. They paused to speak briefly to each other before they made their presence known by a firm rat-a-tat-bang on the screen door.

It was early evening. The two younger children had gone to bed. Wallace sat at the kitchen table doing homework. Louisa wiped the soapsuds from her arms and threw a dish towel to the boy. "Dry these dishes, please," she said.

Better to have him occupied and out of the way, in case something was coming that she did not want him to hear.

"I'm coming," Louisa called out the window and crossed through the living room to open the door for them.

There they stood, two dignified, black-garbed, bearded men who handed her their hats as they entered. They represented the faith community that had nurtured her. Now she was being tested.

Both were tall and thin and seemed to be all angles after they seated themselves in the chairs she indicated to them. Elder Specht leaned forward in his chair and spoke softly, as though he genuinely cared about her and wanted to make the session as easy for her as possible.

Elder Kruetzer sat straight as a poker and seemed to hold himself aloof, although he participated in the conversation equally. He was a man to whom duty, tradition, and the letter of the law was of supreme importance. His whole aura was accusatory, even before they started to talk. Perhaps he knew less of love and forgiveness, thought Louisa, than his companion.

Whatever the case, the two men wasted no time on small talk, but began immediately to question Louisa in a way that made her pounding heart pound harder still.

"Is it true," asked Elder Specht, "that your husband is still living?"

Thinking of the legal paper that the judge had given her, Louisa replied, "I have no husband."

Elder Specht sighed, and then Elder Kreutzer spoke sternly:

"Were you married to Amos Hochstetler?"

"Yes."

"And is Amos Hochstetler still alive?"

Softly, "Yes."

"And are you divorced from him?"

More softly yet, "Yes."

"On what grounds was this divorce granted?"

"I sought the divorce on the grounds of adultery and gross neglect of duty." Louisa cringed inwardly as she said it because she hated those words.

It was clear that the ministers were not satisfied with Louisa's answer. Elder Kreutzer spoke again. "Mrs. Hochstetler, I did not ask you on what grounds you *sought* the divorce. I asked you on what grounds it was *granted.*"

There was a terrible, uncomfortable silence in the room— a silence which settled down around the three of them until Louisa felt she would smother.

"Well?" Even the gentler voice of Elder Specht was quite insistent.

Louisa took a deep breath and held it before she answered. "It was granted . . . because of neglect."

That did it. If adultery had been proven in court and the divorce granted on that basis, the elders might have accepted the fact of the divorce and loved her anyway, and forgiven her.

Elder Specht sank back in his chair. Elder Kreutzer seemed stiffer than ever.

"Then I think," said the latter, "that you have been attending worship under false pretenses. We will need to take this matter up with the congregation."

They rose, retrieved their hats, and prepared to leave.

Elder Specht paused at the door. "I would advise you to confer with us before you present yourself at the church for worship again." There was sorrow in his voice, almost as if he might have wept for her, might have considered her a sheep gone astray from his flock.

"Come," said the other elder. "Let's be on our way."

And they were gone.

Louisa did not confer with them. There was no need. She knew what their decision would be. She was no longer a part of their world.

Twice in her long life there were periods when Louisa did not attend church faithfully every Sunday. Now she was old, in the nursing home, and no one came for her. The other was after the visit of the elders.

They robbed her of her second greatest pleasure. She missed the worship services terribly. Sunday morning brought a strange, lonely emptiness to her heart. But her first joy, a friendship with Jesus and the assurance of his abiding presence and love, could not be taken away.

After a while, a Methodist neighbor asked if she could take the children to Sunday school with her, and Louisa let them go. She went a few times herself and was welcomed. But it wasn't the same as belonging. Once a Mennonite, always a Mennonite, and she was never quite able to understand why her own church could not accept her when these others did.

7

CHRIS

After sixteen years of trying to support her family on her own—and doing pretty well at it—change came into Louisa's life—and it became better. Much better.

It was late in 1918 when Clem Hertzler's wife died. Louisa's children were grown, married, and gone. Gradually the family had returned to the good graces of the people of Pandora. Only a few women still drew their skirts away from her when they passed. Only a few men looked at her with a knowing leer that indicated that they saw her as a loose woman. Although her church and most influential members still avoided her, Louisa had nursed many townspeople during childbirth, sickness, and death. Her love for them and her gift of herself to them had won her a place again. If she was not completely respected by everyone, at least she was acknowledged by most as a woman of worth to the community.

It was the tenth of October, a fine Indian summer day, when Tolly Ansbarger came racing up in front of Louisa's house in his father's buggy. Louisa was between jobs. Nobody in the community was sick enough to need her nursing care, and she knew of no expected births until later in the month or in November.

Thirteen-year-old Tolly tied his reins to a bush in the yard and ran for the front door. He started pounding on it before he noticed Louisa with the door halfway open waiting for him. When he saw her, he mumbled a quiet, "Oh," blushed and stopped to catch his breath before he spoke.

"Miz Hochstetler, you're needed out to the Hertzler place, iffen you can come."

Tolly answered the question on her face without her asking. "Miz Hertzler took a fall in the barn. Dr. Neiswander is already on his way out, and he said I should come by for you." He hesitated. "It was a very bad fall, ma'am. Some of them think she may not live. With all them little kids and all, you may be needed for quite a spell."

Again there was a pause. Tolly ducked his head. "Clem says he reckons he is able to arrange payment just as well as the next man, ma'am . . . but it might take him a little longer is all."

"Oh, no . . . ," said Louisa. "He mustn't think about that at all. Of course I'll come. You wait until I get my things."

"Will that be long, ma'am?"

"Only a minute, Tolly. I keep a bag packed."

And they were off down the road behind Ansbargers' bay mare.

Anna Hertzler died early the next morning just as the first sun was beginning to sift earthward from the top of the sky.

Louisa stayed to take care of the children, cook, and make herself generally useful with household chores.

Chris arrived the day before his sister's funeral, and he, too, stayed—to help his brother-in-law with the farm work.

For the rest of her life, Louisa was able to close her eyes and see Chris as he was that first time.

She had stepped off the enclosed back porch at the Hertzlers' with a basket full of wet wash to hang on the line, banging the screen door closed behind her.

Chris did not see her when he walked out of the darkness of the barn into the light of the dooryard. He was looking at his hands, held out in front of him, covered with some kind of muck from the barn, and at the pump, where he was headed.

It was as if something inside Louisa walked out of darkness and into light at that moment as well—a premonition of what that particular man would one day mean to her. Her heart thumped a dance of joy, and she felt a warm blush rush to her cheeks.

Snorting at her own folly, she set the basket of wash by the steps and turned back into the house to avoid the meeting and to regain her composure.

Don't be a fool, she told herself sharply. *You don't have to look at every man you see as a prospective husband!* This self-accusation came despite the fact that she had not made a habit of seeing the men she met in such a light. Remarriage had never seemed much of a possibility. *Why, you're an old woman compared to him. He can't be a day over forty.*

Another thought struck her then, and she shook her head, as if in apology. *And probably married, too. Louisa Hochstetler, what has come over you!*

She straightened her apron, rolled up a sleeve that had started to slide, and turned back to the basket of clothes.

They met at dinner, after Clem Hertzler had told her to set another place at table. "My brother-in-law, Christian Basinger, is here. He came this morning. I reckon he'll be staying awhile, to help out on the place until," his voice faltered, and there seemed to be tears caught in his throat. "You know," was all he could say.

They would have eaten in silence, except that Louisa felt that conversation might make things easier for Clem. She asked questions of Chris and the children, and let Clem talk or be silent, according to his mood.

Chris was staying in the barn since Louisa occupied the only extra room in the house, which was why she had not seen him when he arrived.

"Why, I could move in with the children," Louisa offered. "The girls have an extra bed in their room."

"No," said Chris. "No, you don't need to do that." Actually, he seemed rather pleased with the situation. "There's something special about crawling into bed in a nice, warm barn with the smell of hay, and one of Clem's old cows talking to you, and sometimes the sound of rain on the roof."

It was then she learned that he was a bachelor at forty. "Never did find the kind of woman I wanted," he said. "Never cared for those giddy young things that'd simper and giggle and jump to look pretty just because there was a man around."

"No," he went on, holding his cup for more coffee when Louisa offered it, "I'd have wanted me a woman who was strong and knew how to take care of herself—and maybe me if I needed it sometimes. I wouldn't even have minded if she was a little bossy. I think I could've learnt to handle that.

"A woman like that could put a little spice in a man's life," he finished, grinning around the table at them.

He smiled a lot, one way or another. Sometimes it was a lopsided grin, and his eyes would sparkle. Sometimes it was a soft turning up of his mouth at the corners with more gentleness and love in his eyes than laughter.

After the funeral they both stayed on. It was understood that Clem and the children needed them.

Gradually—Louisa had to stop and think about it later in order to realize it had happened—Chris began spending a lot of time in her kitchen. He came for coffee at odd hours. He seemed to know by instinct when she had heavy work to do. He would stand in the doorway, waiting for her to notice him, then do the heavy chores for her.

When the smell of fresh bread floated out into the crisp air of the dooryard on those late fall days, he would come to claim a thick-sliced end from one of the crusty loaves, talking with her while he spread a layer of butter and strawberry jam, telling her how he liked hot bread right out of the oven. "But not milk," he said. "Can't eat a thing with milk in it. Can't even put cream in my coffee—though I like the taste of it powerful well. There's something in milk that upsets my system real bad."

And one day when Louisa was having a problem with one of the children, Chris was suddenly there.

"Nellie, I want you to set the table now," Louisa said to the oldest girl, who was seven.

The child's eyes turned dark and her lips twisted downward. "Ain't gonna do it," she said. "Don't have to. Never had to do such stuff when Mama was here."

Louisa turned to her, wondering whether anger or kindness was the best answer for the child, when suddenly the back door opened and shut again in time for Chris to catch the last of the impertinent words.

"Nellie," he said, pulling off his coat. "Come here, please."

Chris pulled a chair away from the table, sat down in it, and took the little girl in his lap. "Nell," he said, "we can't have such talk. It's not pleasin' to me or to Miz Hochstetler. It's not pleasin' to your pa. It's not pleasin' to our Lord Jesus."

The child ducked her head. She was chewing on the end of one long braid as she listened. The argument did not seem to convince her.

"And it wouldn't . . . " Chris took a deep breath, " . . . it wouldn't be pleasin' to your ma, either."

Nellie sniffed and mumbled past the braid, "I got no ma."

"Yes, you do," said Chris. "She was hurtin' too bad to stay here with us. The good Lord took her with him, so's she wouldn't have to hurt anymore. But she's still your ma." He put a firm hand under Nellie's chin and tipped her face toward him so he could look into her eyes. "And someday . . . I don't know just how long, but someday . . . we'll all go to be with her.

"Now when that happens, Nellie Hertzler, do you want to have to tell your ma you been sassin' Miz Hochstetler?"

"No, sir, Uncle Chris."

"Well then," he said, "you get on about the business of bein' the kind of woman your ma will be pleased to meet whenever you get together again."

"Yes, sir."

He pulled the child to him and hugged her tightly, as if he would impart some strength of his own into the tiny, sorrowing body. "And the rest of us, we're gonna do everything we can to help you," he promised.

Nellie climbed off his lap, sliding down his knee to the floor, and started for the cupboard to get the plates. She paused for only a moment. "You're sure she's all right, and I'm gonna see her again . . . someday?" she asked, turning back.

"I'm sure, Nellie."

Oh, thought Louisa, watching the scene from the corner of her eye while she went on about dinner. *The gentleness of the man!* Her own pa had been kind enough whenever he stayed home. Amos had shown kindness enough when he chose. But not like this.

Louisa had never known a man like this quiet, smiling, handsome Christian Basinger.

At first she didn't do much thinking about the fact that he kept coming into the kitchen so much more often than anyone else. She was fifty years old, after all.

One afternoon she caught him looking at her, studying her features as if he thought to read there what she was thinking, and looking beyond, to the deep places of her soul. He grinned when she caught him, but he didn't seem embarrassed.

Accidental eavesdropping first let her know what was in his mind. She had gone out early on a windy, snowy morning to collect eggs. It was, as a matter of fact, much earlier than when she usually did that chore, and Chris was still in the barn after milking the cows.

No one else was usually about at that hour, so when she passed the barn door and heard him talking, she leaned in to see who might be with him.

"Now, Lord," he said, "I want to talk to you about Louisa . . . Miz Hochstetler . . . . "

It was one of the most deeply moving experiences of Louisa's life.

She wasn't wholly surprised later, then, when he came to her and said, "Now, Louisa . . . Miz Hochstetler . . . I want to talk to you about the Lord—and about something I think he maybe has in mind for us."

Many people in Pandora were shocked when Louisa and Chris were married. They couldn't understand how she could remarry. The divorce, they said over their back fences, was bad enough—but to take another husband afterward? Really!

Louisa had not realized that there were so many different ways to say the word.

"Really?"

"Really?"

"REALLY?!?"

Her marriage was hardest for Wallace. Hurting, he came back to town one day before the wedding, to sit talking in the kitchen and to ask her to change her mind. "It's against the word, Ma," he said. "It's against God's word." Bewilderment and pain were in his eyes as he leaned forward across the table toward her.

Wallace even talked to the minister who was to marry them. "How can you do this?" he demanded of the man.

"Ma," he said later, "that preacher didn't have any answers for me, but he's going to go through with it for you." Wallace left town again, shaking his head, still bewildered and hurt.

It was not that Wallace didn't like Chris. He did, but it was just that he thought what he believed was right, and he could not change.

Louisa fought a battle with herself over the whole thing.

Out of a religious and family background that taught that divorce was sin, she had dared to believe that there were exceptions to the rule. She had acted on her beliefs to protect her children and herself.

Now came Chris, and a question about something else she had been taught was sin: remarriage after divorce.

Round and round she went, with the Lord—and with the inner Louisa.

"God, my Father . . . *is* it sin?"

"God, I never wanted anything in my life but to serve you well. I never sinned against that. I wasn't the one who ran away. I was faithful to my husband."

"God, must I be punished the rest of my life because someone did something wrong to me and to my children, and I had to try to set it right?"

"God, if this was not supposed to be, why did you let me meet Chris at all? Why did you let me love him?"

There were dicussions in the town, some people taking one side, and some the other:

A friend said, "Why not? I don't see anything wrong with it."

An aunt whose very words were, "You make me sick to my stomach, Louisa Hochstetler. If you're going to do a thing like that, I wish I'd never had to know about it."

A neighbor questioned, "Getting married again? Well, I don't know . . . . "

Some of the comments made her feel terrible, but none of them helped with the decision. It was hers to make, and she had to make it alone.

When Chris entered the argument, she realized she wasn't so alone after all.

Late one evening toward spring, they sat on her porch steps, talking about what life had been like for them. He sat with his elbows on his knees, his clasped hands extended out in front of him, and his head bowed in what was almost an attitude of prayer.

After a long silence beneath the stars, he turned to her. "Louisa, dear," he said. "You need one good man in your life who will do right by you." For a moment, he seemed uncomfortable, as if he thought that sounded like boasting.

"Well . . . I know I'm not perfect. But I . . . I would like to take care of you . . . make you a home where you can be at home and do the things you like—keep house, cook, sew— for someone who loves you, instead of for someone who is paying you to do it, or someone whose love is so weak he's going to run off and leave you. That's how God meant for people to be.

"I believe God sent me to you for that. I surely do. Louisa, I have to live by what *I* believe. I can't live some other way, just because some other person thinks that what they believe is better."

There was a long pause then, and Chris bowed his head again. "And if I'm wrong," he said, "then please, God, forgive me."

Louisa reached a gentle hand to touch his shirt sleeve. "Us," she corrected. "If *we* are wrong, then God forgive *us*."

And so Louisa and Chris were married. They moved into the little house on Monroe Street, where they spent many happy years. They became members of the Missionary Church, an evangelical group with ties to the Mennonite tradition. Here they were welcomed and loved.

8

MY CHILDREN ... MY FRIENDS

At the Parmenter County Nursing Home, many friends, too, walked across the stage of Louisa's life in her last years. Many were relatives—mostly descendants, because everyone from her own generation was already gone.

Some of them were close friends.

Some of them, in touching her heart, hardly even noticed what they had done for her.

A woman and a little girl, for example, came one day to visit someone else, and even that was pleasant. It was early afternoon, and most of the residents were in the day room. The woman sat beside a man in a wheelchair, talking earnestly, while the child danced about the room, peering warily into ancient faces.

Louisa watched the little girl, fascinated.

"Hello," the child chirped over and over. "What's your name?"

Sometimes she got an answer—"Bert," or "Julia," or "George." Just as often, she did not. Either way, she moved on.

A few of the residents ignored the child. Most of them, loving her presence, followed her progress with hungry eyes, as if she were some wondrous thing that provided nourishment for their souls.

One woman cried out, "A little girl! Ohhhhhh! It's been so *long* since I've seen a little girl .... It's so *good* to see a little girl again!" There were delighted tears on her plump, wrinkled cheeks.

Suddenly there was an agonized, frightened shriek. The child bounced up and down in one spot, crying, "Mama!"

A wrinkled hag in a wheel chair had crept up behind the girl and entwined her knotty fingers in the child's hair. By jerking on the hair, she brought the tiny, struggling form closer and closer to her lap.

"Hold you? Please! Hold you?" begged the cracked mouth, while the little girl fought on and wept.

Louisa would have helped if she could. She was close enough and started to struggle out of her chair. The movement caught the child's eye, and new fear sprang to her face.

When Louisa placed her hand on the railing to pull herself up, she suddenly understood that new fear. She could not help but notice that her own hand was like the hand of the assailant.

A bitter sadness washing over her in waves, Louisa realized that there was nothing she could do to help. To the child she would seem as ancient and frightening as the other. She sank back onto her cushions and wearily, with pain in her heart and soul, she watched the mother move to the rescue.

Some of her descendants brought their children, too.

They brought them to stare wide-eyed at her. "This is your great-great-grandmother, Tommy. Say hello."

If the child were old enough to be embarrassed by it all, he mumbled an awkward "Hello" and retreated.

The younger ones shyly clung to their mothers' legs and said nothing at all.

They brought their children to boast. "Gramma, Paula is really doing well in school this year. She says now she wants to be a teacher." Laughter. "She must take after Grandpa Wallace."

They brought them for her blessing.

The granddaughter from Nebraska came with four. "Hello, Gramma," she said, with the children standing, well-mannered, like stair steps beside her.

It was disconcerting at first. Here again was a woman Louisa did not know, walking up to her and saying, "Hello,

Gramma." She puzzled, trying to recall if this was someone she had seen before.

The woman spoke again, and Louisa remembered: Geraldine's girl—the older. The other one had died years ago in an automobile accident. This was a great-granddaughter, then. The children were great-greats.

There was silence in the room after that. But it was not an empty silence. There seemed to be something of reverence in it, as though God graced the moment with his presence.

The great-granddaughter from Nebraska sat on the bed, reached out, and took Louisa's hand. She seemed to want to say something, but her eyes were damp with tears, and her lips trembled. So she sat and clung to the hand, as if she hoped some message might be transmitted from her heart to Louisa's.

I have come, the granddaughter was thinking, *into the presence of a godly woman, and it is an awesome thing.* She was also thinking about the loneliness and the boredom of the nursing home, and about her grandmother's sturdy love of independence . . . and work . . . and home.

Louisa never knew those thoughts, so she never quite understood the strange, silent woman who sat on her bed and wept for her.

When she could finally talk, the granddaughter said only, "The children, Gramma. Please . . . give the children your blessing."

The four came to kneel by her chair. She placed her hands on each bowed head in turn. She let the hands rest on each one for a moment, thinking, "How did this happen? Where did the years go? And my youth and strength? Why am I suddenly the only one left of my generation in this family? I am the oldest, and they bring the children to me for blessing. How can this be?"

But it was. And since it was, she gave herself to them. A part of her was somehow broken off and given to the children. No word was spoken, but the room was filled with prayer.

Experiences like that were encouraging to Louisa. She was content in knowing that when she left the world she would leave behind descendants who loved her God as much as she did. A part of her purpose in life was fulfilled in giving them to the world.

It was as if the children, by their coming, had given her a gift of tangible joy that she could hold close to her heart.

She tried always, in the rest home, as she had done in the little house on Monroe Street, to give tangibly to the children, too.

It was harder, of course. In the Monroe Street house, she had always had a box of little toys for them to play with. In room 34, the best she could do was a battered puzzle in a frame tray, a stringy-haired doll, a tiny, red fire truck with chipped paint, and, of course, the ghastly purple elephant that Louisa's adult visitors usually deplored.

Perhaps it was not so strange that the children liked it as well as Louisa did.

Kathy was the first one of them to take it from its place on the windowsill.

"Kathy have it? Kathy have?" the child had asked, pointing to the fuzzy, pink tusks during a Sunday afternoon visit.

"No-no." her mother had answered, pushing the tiny, pointing finger aside and taking the child into her arms. "That's Gramma's."

Louisa, who had been about to deny the treasure herself, caught just a hint of the little girl's whimper of disappointment and spoke her compassion for a child's need.

"Let her have it," she said.

Then and at other times the very young and the very old in room 34 joined forces.

Once it was the purple elephant.

Another time it was a cookie. "No, Gramma, she shouldn't have one now," the mother had said.

But when the mother wasn't looking, Louisa had slipped the child a cookie anyhow and got away with it.

Yet another time it was bouncing on the bed. "Get down from there!" the mother had ordered, and a little fellow in blue jeans sighed and climbed off the little town on the bed spread.

It was not long before Louisa stood as if to stretch and went and sat on the bed herself. Shortly she called that same little fellow up beside her, and they both bounced. Not much, but enough.

Louisa always had a feeling that she probably shouldn't do things like that, but she did them. After nearly a century of living, it felt good to side with the young again. It felt very good.

There were many other things about her visitors that made her feel good.

Young visitors gave her a chance to share the wisdom she had gathered in a century of living. There were so many important things that young people just didn't seem to know about anymore.

When Tammy was pregnant, Louisa was there to tell her about the importance of avoiding any exercise that would cause her stomach muscles to contract too hard or too fast, and about the danger of stretching to reach something high, because either of those things could cause the cord to become tangled around the baby's neck.

When Tammy's baby son was born, red, squalling, and healthy, Louisa felt she had made a contribution to the successful birthing of one more descendant.

One day when a lot of family was there, Louisa was able to warn them about an impending storm and send them home in time to miss the worst of it.

They were in the day room with her on a Sunday afternoon, sitting and chatting among themselves, except for the children, who tended either to wander aimlessly or to hop, depending upon their age. For an hour or so, Louisa had been watching the herd of cows she could see from the window, and finally she mentioned them.

"Chris," she said, leaning toward him, "Look at those cows. Don't they act to you like there's a storm brewing?"

He turned to watch for a while. The animals seemed restless, sniffing the air. Then they clustered together and began settling into beds they had chosen along the fence row.

"Oh, yeah," said Chris. "There's something coming, all right. Cows lying down in the pasture this time of day . . . there's sure to be something coming.

"And besides," he added, "see how the smoke out of that chimney yonder is settling down to the ground, instead of rising like it should?"

Louisa hadn't noticed that. Her eyes weren't what they should be anymore. But now that Chris mentioned it, it confirmed what she was thinking.

"Wallace," she said firmly. "Wallace, I think you folks ought to head off home."

Wallace looked up, puzzled, from where he was playing with one of his granddaughters. So did a couple of the others who had overheard.

"Why, Ma?" he asked. "It's Sunday afternoon. I was planning to spend a couple more hours with you at least."

"No, Wallace, I want you should be going now. There's going to be a good storm, and you're better off not having to drive in that kind of weather."

One of the younger ones questioned her pronouncement. "How do you know?"

"Look at those cows," she said. "Any one knows you see cows acting like that, it's going to get bad out. And the smoke from that chimney is going to the ground," she added, hoping that Chris was right. Since she couldn't see for herself, she'd just have to trust him.

They peered through the cloudy afternoon at the cows and the smoke, shrugged their shoulders and went, with disbelief, but willing to humor her.

Most of them got home before the storm struck, and Louisa was pleased about that.

Sometimes, though, they didn't listen to her advice, which worried her considerably.

Tommy stopped in one day with his mama. He was wearing only one shoe. The other foot was bandaged, and covered with a heavy sock.

"Well, what ever happened to you, boy?" asked Louisa.

Tommy grinned and mumbled a soft answer that Louisa couldn't quite catch.

"He stepped on a nail," his mama answered for him. "We've been to the doctor and got him a tetanus shot, and he's fine."

"Doesn't look too fine to me," said Louisa. "Looks a mite peaked." She waved a wrinkled hand and summoned the fourteen-year-old to her side, where she peered worriedly into his face, and bent to examine the bandaged foot.

"You know," Louisa asked, "You know when I was younger, what we used to do if a body stepped on a nail?"

Neither of them said anything, and she went on. "We used to take them right away and soak that foot in a pan of warm cow manure—steaming, you know."

"I know," said Tommy's mama. "But this is a better way, the shot and all. He's all right. Really, Gramma." There was a touch of chagrin in the mama's voice, as if she wished the old woman would drop the subject.

"If it was me," Louisa continued, undaunted, "I think maybe I'd do both. Some of those old remedies had a lot of power to them."

"Yes," she said, nodding. "I think I'd do both, just to be on the safe side.

"What do you think of that, Tom?" she finished, turning to the youngster.

Tommy's fourteen-year-old face lit up with a completely uncontrollable grin, as if he knew in advance that the thing he was about to say was going to get his mother and great-great-grandmother really riled, and as if the temptation was beyond resisting.

"Gee, Gramma," he said. "The doctor told me that people used to do that when you stepped on a nail." The grin spread crazily across his face to reach out to every part of his sturdy young body. "But then the doctor also said . . . that if they did that to a kid, he was never worth a crap afterwards."

"Thomas Shaffer!" shouted his mother "You apologize to your Gramma and go sit in the car."

"Sorry, Gramma," said Tommy, still grinning and obviously not too repentant.

But he left them with something to talk about at least.

"What are kids coming to these days?" asked Louisa, shaking her head.

"I wonder," said Tommy's mother, shaking her head. "I sure never said things like that around *my* mother."

"I never said things like that at all," said Louisa.

There were other times, though, when Louisa's advice—even her home-remedy-type medical advice—went over better. A three-year-old visitor got stung by a bee that was making a nuisance of itself in room 34.

"Oh, dear," said the child's mother. "I wish I had something to put on it to take away the sting." And she rushed to the bathroom to begin running cold water over the small white spot.

Louisa, though, knew what to do. Reaching for the potted chrysanthemum on her window sill, she took several leaves and crushed them until the juice ran on her fingers.

"Bring her here," Louisa said. Reluctant to give up the cold running water, the mother brought the crying child to Louisa.

The old woman dried the sting with the hem of her dress, then began gently rubbing the juice of the leaves onto the spot.

Within minutes, the child was on her lap, saying softly, "More do, Gramma. Is better now. More do," and holding up the injured arm for application of more juice.

I hope, thought Louisa, *that all of them will remember this the next time it happens.*

It felt good—oh, so good—to be able to help with something like that.

There were other experiences that she had mixed feelings about; she couldn't quite decide whether she liked them or not.

Louisa had never been one for making a fuss, but when she became one hundred, and they celebrated her birthday, they made *such* a fuss!

And when she and Chris reached their fiftieth wedding anniversary, and all the folks discovered that it was her second marriage at that, they made a *terrible* fuss.

It was nice, in a way, to have the attention. But it was an uncommon thing for Louisa, and she had to admit to herself that a part of her was uncomfortable with it.

And there were some things that Louisa just couldn't feel good about at all.

A simple thing like a trip down the hall, for example, could be a good experience—or an awful one.

When people were smiling and friendly as she made her way slowly along in the walker, it was a good experience.

There were other kinds of people, though, visitors and the unthinking orderlies who acted as if she were not a person at all.

"Out of the way, old one," one might say, as if he were making a joke. "I've got to mop this floor."

Or, "Don't you know you're supposed to be in your room, getting ready for bed!"

Or, "I hate coming here. I just hate it! All these *old* people!"

Or, with a slight curling of the lip, "Why do old folks *smell* so bad?"

Or, "It must be terrible to be that old. Just *terrible!*"

The cruel words made Louisa cling closer to the wall as she walked, almost as if she might become part of the building and lose some of the disgrace of growing old. Old buildings, provided they were maintained well, were granted more dignity and honor than old people.

The words of unthinking visitors always had that effect on her until Jessie stepped in.

Jessie followed Louisa down the hall one day and watched her trembling and shrinking closer to the wall. She rolled her wheelchair beside the old woman clutching the walker.

"Louisa," she said. "Louisa Basinger, I want to talk to you."

Louisa stopped and turned to face Jessie, whose wheelchair now stood beside her.

"You stop listening to them," she said firmly. As she talked, her fingers went to Louisa's arm and straightened the place where Louisa's sweater was rumpled. "I see what they're doing to you. And you've got to stop listening to them." Her voice was more than firm, almost angry.

Louisa looked back, not knowing how the pain she felt inside could show on the outside.

"You are one hell of a woman, Louisa Basinger . . . one hell of a woman!"

Louisa winced at the words, as if they had been rocks thrown at her. *Dear Lord, I know she means well. But will the woman never learn to watch her tongue?*

Jessie continued. "Just because these dummies don't understand doesn't mean you have to accept their opinion of you. You remember that!" She left Louisa to translate the statement into words she could accept.

"She thinks I'm a good woman," thought Louisa, staring after her. "She thinks I'm a strong woman and she thinks I'm worthwhile." Shoulders straightened, she raised her chin as she moved away from the wall.

It doesn't matter what other people think. They don't know. They've never been old yet, and you can't really understand a thing like this until you've been here. So it doesn't matter what they think. All that really matters is what God and I think of me.

Well, she added, *and maybe Chris, too.*

Louisa's step was different after that, as she made her way through the halls. She remembered what Jessie had said whenever unpleasantness came from the younger family members. Like the day Louisa and Chris visited Wallace at home and Chris forgot his hat.

Everyone made it a sign of his aging. "Chris is getting old. His memory is starting to go," they said, whispering among themselves. Louisa remembered Jessie and was no longer hurt by their unthinking words.

A month or so later, when Wallace forgot *his* hat on a visit to room 34, nobody gave it a second thought.

There were many times when she needed that particular advice that Jessie had given: when they had lessons in the day room, for example.

Louisa thought the lessons were awful.

"Come on, everybody," the activities director would call out, "tell me what day it is."

Some indistinct mutterings would come in response, and then the director would say, "That's right! It's Thursday! Everybody say it together now, big and loud: It's Thur-r-r-sday. That's right."

Louisa thought that there were probably some who needed that kind of mental exercise. Some of the residents wouldn't remember five minutes later what day it was, not even if she went over it a hundred times.

But for Louisa, lesson time always seemed like some kind of strange, planned insult to her intelligence. She was tempted, not only to retreat into the past, but to stay there.

She looked across at Chris, who was busy repeating "March 30" after the activities director, and knew why she couldn't allow herself to live in the past, although others might.

The activities director was making an announcement. "We have something special for you today. A group of young people called 'That's Life.' They are going to make some music for us."

Louisa and the other residents turned toward the front room, where several young men with guitars and drums and a girl in blue jeans were walking in.

Oh, dear, thought Louisa. *Oh, dear. The music this younger generation makes! I suppose I'll have to sit and listen to it. As slow as I get around these days, they'll be gone before I can get up and out anyhow.*

The program started as Louisa had feared it would—a little too loud, songs she'd never heard, and a way of singing she couldn't quite appreciate.

But after half an hour or so, they set the guitars in holders and began to move around the room. They held hands, patted shoulders, and they took time to talk to persons who could respond.

It was the girl in blue jeans and a long-haired, pony-tailed boy who came, after a time, to Louisa.

Humph! thought Louisa. But she answered them politely, and in a moment, the "humph!" had turned to quiet respect.

"Hello," the girl said. "What's your name?"

"Basinger," said Louisa. "I'm Louisa. He's Chris."

"Do you like our music?" asked the girl.

Louisa started to lie to her and say, "I like it fine." The lie wouldn't come, not even for the sake of good manners. She started again.

"It's not quite what I'm used to."

The girl smiled gently. "What *are* you used to, Mrs. Basinger?"

"Oh," said Louisa, hesitating as she remembered the last time she had tried to tell someone about her favorite music. "Oh . . . mostly hymns, I guess. Mostly . . . " Louisa hesitated, searching the girl's face for the laughter that she expected. It wasn't there.

" . . . mostly I like songs about my Lord."

The long-haired boy interrupted. "What's your favorite?"

Again Louisa hesitated, her heart pumping hard in anticipation of their scorn. She found it hard to say but finally, as she studied them, it came. " 'Lead Kindly Light,' " she whispered softly. "Oh, I do like that one so much—and so does Chris."

They smiled, the girl squeezed her hand, and they left her.

Well, thought Louisa, *at least they didn't laugh at me.*

But the amazing thing was that the musical group came again a few weeks later.

"Now," said the girl, as she announced their songs, "we want to sing some things that you like especially."

For a moment, Louisa hoped. *Forget it,* she told herself. *They won't.*

They sang, "Put on your Old Gray Bonnet," "Down by the Old Mill Stream," and a lot of other old, familiar tunes. At the very end of their program, the girl said, "This song is for Louisa and Chris. We aren't used to playing this kind of music, and it took us some time to learn it, but we hope you like it."

She smiled then, right at Louisa and Chris. The guitars and voices began softly: "Lead, kindly light, amid th'encircling gloom . . . "

It wasn't the kind of song that usually was accompanied by guitars and drums. It did sound different that way. But they *did* it; that was the important thing.

Oh, thought Louisa. *It's beautiful. And so are they.*

When the hymn was ended, the six young people came to hug her. Her tears fell on their denim shirts and on their own cheeks, but they didn't even notice.

I don't like this place, thought Louisa, watching them go. *I'd much rather be home. I have to admit, though, that some good things do happen here.*

Basically, she thought that living in the nursing home was like most of the rest of her life had been—both good and bad.

In spite of the spiritual pain Louisa had learned to know at Parmenter County, life there was not all bad.

Although there had been frequent pain in her growing-up years, it had not been a hard life always then, either, Louisa had taken with her into young womanhood many pleasant memories.

When she grew old, she kept quiet about her hard life, unless someone encouraged her to talk about it. But she loved to remember spelling bees, covered bridges, and bobsled trips to church.

One of her favorite memories was of the old-time tradition of visiting for dinner after Sunday services. "I remember one time . . . ," she would say, shaking her head, while laughter added to the wrinkles at her eyes and mouth. " . . . I remember one time where we had more than *forty* for dinner . . . " Here she would pause for effect before finishing her sentence. " . . . and the folks didn't even know we were *coming* after church."

Nobody had gone hungry, either. First smiling, and then laughing, Mama had watched the crowd that followed her children through the front door.

The boys and men clustered around Papa—Papa, who did not go to church with them, but who always put on clean overalls for Sunday, and who loved company even more than the rest of them.

Mama began to assign duties to the women and girls.

There were homemade bread and fresh strawberries, hard-boiled eggs, pressed chicken, boiled potatoes, *schmierkase,* smoked ham, fresh milk, and all kinds of sweets and sours from the pantry. On and on had gone the list of country dishes Mama had come up with on the spur of the moment. Their guests had eaten well that day.

No, not all of life was hard for young Louisa Nussbaum. And not all of life was hard for the old Louisa, either. She left her old friends in memory, where they belonged, and returned again from past to present—more willingly this time.

She would have preferred to be in her own home, but room 34 was what she had. It would have to do.

"There are good times yet to come," she thought contentedly.

But Louisa didn't realize that the worst thing—the very worst thing of all—was yet to happen to her.

9

LOSING A BEST FRIEND

"What do *you* do, mister?" A high-pitched, childish voice rang out across the day room. From beneath a thatch of white-blonde hair, mischievous blue eyes peered up at Chris.

From beneath a thatch of white-gray hair, far older eyes peered back. The high-pitched voice and the scene that followed put a look of pain in those eyes.

The child—six or seven years old—had been scrambling about the floor, playing with a plastic train. In the cluster of adults around him, talk turned to trains and engineers and then to other jobs.

"What's an engineer?" said the child. One of the old men explained.

"Had an Uncle Jake who used to be an engineer," said another of the men.

"One of my uncles used to ride trains a lot, too," a third man spoke as he grinned a fantastic, toothy smile. "But he sure wasn't no engineer." He paused, waiting for the rest of them to raise questioning eyebrows, before he finished, "He was a 'bo!"

Delighted laughter drew them together as if they had reached out to wrap their arms around each other.

"What's a 'bo?" asked the child.

Explanations were again given.

"And I'm an orderly," said a young fellow with a push cart, joining the conversation.

"What's an orderly?" said the child. The young fellow told him.

"What do you do?" The child's blue eyes turned to the man beside Chris who turned away and would not—or could not—answer.

Puzzled, the child tried again. "Hey, mister!" But there was still no answer.

The blue eyes fell on Chris, and the painful question was asked again, innocently.

"What do you *do,* mister?"

From across the room, a booming male voice, stern, over-powering in the certainty of its own rightness, held the attention of everyone in the room.

"Buddy," said the voice. "Get away from there and leave those people alone. They don't *do* anything. They're too old."

Chris blinked rapidly, as if his eyelids might ward off the verbal blow. It was too late. The stinging words had sunk deep into him, and there was no cure for that.

I don't do anything, he thought. *I'm too old, and I don't do anything.*

Beside him, another old man began to weep, tiny rivulets of tears winding their way down his cracked and wrinkled cheeks to drop like miniature waterfalls from his jaw and soak gently into his plaid flannel shirt.

On the other hand, a third man began to mutter. "I *used* to do something. I had a farm once . . . and a herd of dairy cows. And later—during the war—I worked in a defense plant, and I got a letter from the President saying how good I done. I got three of them letters. They're in my room now. I could show them to you."

He looked around hopefully. "Anybody want to see my letter from the President?" No one heard him—or if they did, they paid no attention.

The man sighed. "They're awfully nice letters," he said.

Chris wasn't listening. He stood slowly, struggling for balance. "I don't *do* anything," he said.

That thought bent and folded his body even more as he slowly shuffled out.

He went down the hall toward the room he had come to call home, and toward his wife of nearly fifty years.

"Louisa," he called softly as he approached the door. "Louisa, dear . . . where are you?"

Something in his bent body, his shuffle, and his soft call caught the attention of one of the nurses.

"Well, Mr. B.," she said, taking his arm. "What's the matter?"

"I don't *do* anything," he said again, turning watery eyes to her. "I used to be a person . . . but now I'm not anything."

"Of course you are," the nurse answered. "You're Chris Basinger." She smiled. "And you're one of my favorite people." She patted him on the shoulder, then reached a gentle hand to touch his hair back into place in a gesture that was meant to be pure comfort.

At that precise moment, Louisa stepped out of the door. "Were you calling me," she started to say.

Instead her eyes saw the pat and the touch. Her glance turned cold as it took in the two of them, the old man and the woman in white.

"Well," said Louisa. "Well . . . well . . . well." There was hurt in the way she said the words . . . and anger . . . and love, much love.

He's so handsome, she thought. *So good. I don't blame her. I don't blame her one bit.*

Turning, she went back into the room. When Chris walked through the door, it was very hard to talk to him.

Moments like that happened often while they were in Parmenter County Home. Louisa *knew* that they happened because those young, pretty, soft-spoken nurses must be interested in her handsome husband. It made life even more difficult for her.

Most of the time she stayed near him—and that helped.

I need to be patient with him, she thought. *He's always been so good to me. A woman ought to be able to put up with a little flirting from a man who's always been that good.*

She remembered that most of the time. The pain and the jealousy, sometimes, got too much for her, and she forgot. Then she grumbled.

Her husband was, after all, the best friend she had—after, of course, that one Friend above all others. The loss of Chris's friendship at such a time in her life would have been tragic. She forgave him his "other women" and tried to remember only the good.

Not far into the eight years that Louisa stayed at Parmenter County Nursing Home, however, the tragedy came. Louisa tried to take good care of Chris. She seldom let him eat in the dining room. He seemed so out of place there. Chris was quiet, gentle, handsome, and still in control of his mind and body. She couldn't stand to see him eating among all those old folks with their runny noses, drippy mouths, and stringy hair that always—no matter how short it was kept—managed to get food in it.

They had to eat there at first, of course. But as soon as they were allowed to have some of their own possessions, Louisa asked Wallace and Mary to bring a small table for room 34.

Mary found a tiny table with two drop leaves which, when folded, made it tinier still. Most of the time it sat, folded, against the wall by Chris's bed.

But when the bell rang for meals, Chris would smile, stand up and move slowly around the bed to the wall, pleased that the time for his chore had come.

While he worked, Louisa directed. She *always* directed.

"Be sure you have that little thing pulled clear out, or that leaf'll fall when we put the food on it," she would say.

"Turn my chair a little more toward the table, please."

"Why don't we put that vase of flowers off the dresser in the middle for a centerpiece?"

Finally, "Now you get out of the way, dear, and I'll set the table."

She said the same things almost every time. Chris did them just as she told him. He didn't mind. It was just a habit they had fallen into, and he liked it. It was comfortable, like an old pair of shoes.

When the orderly appeared at the door with the trays of food—if they were lucky, it might still be hot—the table was set, and the two of them were perched on their chairs, like two ancient fledglings in their own private nest.

The first thing Louisa did was to slide the food from the tan institutional dishes onto their own more colorful favorites.

Then she put the rest home dishes onto the trays and hid the trays under the bed out of sight.

After that, she was free to breathe deeply, pour coffee for the two of them, and wait for Chris's quiet blessing, revised from the days on Monroe Street: "Lord, bless this food. Bless the hands that prepared it. And bless the dear hands that placed it here before us."

Their table talk was mostly about the food.

"This meat loaf isn't too bad," Louisa might offer.

Chris would reply, "But it's nowhere near as good as yours." Old as he was, he still had a skill for saying the right words to warm a woman's heart.

Or they might discuss the things they missed most. Food at the rest home was always *so* overcooked. There was no crispness left in anything, and it was texture in their food that they hungered for.

"What I wouldn't give for a couple of good, fresh sweet onions to go with this soup."

Wistfully, while spooning gummy applesauce, "Just once more I'd like to have me a nice, fresh Gravenstein to eat raw."

"You know what this meal needs? It needs a sprig of parsley to finish off with—right straight from the garden. I sure would like that."

Often, they grumbled.

"This soup is well nigh too watery to eat. I wish they'd at least let us have a little extra salt; I can't see where just a dab more would hurt us any."

"Look at this here toast. Mine's white as a sheet, and yours is just plain burned black."

Louisa fussed over Chris, caring for him in other ways, too.

She read to him, sometimes, from the Word that was so precious to them both.

It nearly broke her heart that his laundry was packed into a little plastic bag and sent home with Mary, and she could not do it herself. Sometimes she would keep out a pair of socks or a red handkerchief to wash in the bathroom sink and hang to dry on the back of a chair—to remember the feel of doing laundry for someone she loved.

Other things about his clothes had to be done by someone else, too—ironing and the like. But Louisa was able to do a little mending for him, if someone threaded the needle for her. Sometimes, when she was done sewing on a button, she would hang up the shirt and stand back to look at it as if she had just finished the whole garment. She would try to recapture that special warmth of long ago when she had been able to do such things for him. She experienced a new depth to her sadness, instead. She would shut the closet door on the shirt to put it out of her mind.

That was when Chris was well.

When he was ill, Louisa tried even harder to take care of him.

One night he woke her, calling softly across the darkness between them. "Louisa. Louisa, dear. I need to go to the bathroom. I've rung and rung and the nurse won't come. Do you suppose there's something wrong with our bell?"

Louisa's heart contracted painfully, touched by the fear and loneliness in that dear voice.

He had gone to bed the night before complaining of an upset stomach. From the unpleasant odor that hung thick in the room, she knew that it was more than a stomachache. He had needed help, and no nurse had come in time to spare her beloved husband the embarrassment of a soiled bed.

Dear Lord, don't let him feel too bad about it, she said to herself.

"I'll take care of it," she said aloud, and eased her feet over the edge.

Across the room and down the hall marched Louisa in her blue flannel nightgown thumping her walker ahead of her, her white-gold hair forming a haystack halo, her bare feet slapping softly against the tile floor.

"I need some help," she announced loudly at the nurses' station. "Didn't you hear our bell?"

A startled nurse turned from her records to look at Louisa. "Mrs. B., you are not supposed to be out of bed alone in the night."

Louisa was not intimidated. "I need help and I need it now," she replied. "Come with me, please."

The nurse put one hand on Louisa's shoulder and one hand on the walker to turn the old woman around. She wouldn't turn.

"Come *with* me," said Louisa again. "Now." A sly grin touched her lips and eyes. She knew what the night staff feared the most.

"If you don't . . . . " She let the sentence hang, unfinished, for a moment. Yes, it was a threat—something she probably would never have done for herself. But for Chris . . . ? "If you don't, I'll yell so loud I'll wake every person in every room on this wing." She nodded her head firmly. "I will, too. So there!"

"Mrs. B.!" said the nurse. "Please don't!"

"Then come with me," said Louisa, and turned to march back down the hall toward room 34 with the help she knew would be following.

A woman had to do what she had to do in order to take care of her own.

There came the day when there was no longer anything she could do for Chris.

He had aged much in the weary, hateful days of rest home living. He was thinner. His walk was slower, and his shoulders more stooped. And he could hardly hear at all.

His veined hands and tired voice shook too much.

His eyes sometimes could not distinguish whether it was Louisa across the room from him, or someone else. That last, was the thing that gave him the greatest pain.

"Talk to me when you're around, Louisa, dear," he often said, "so as I can hear your voice and be sure it's you. I need that."

Since he needed it, she did it.

She saw him through a lot before the last days came. There was the attack of diarrhea that so humiliated him, for one thing.

While the aides muttered as they cleaned him up and tidied the room and forgot he was a real person, Louisa sat by his side holding his hand saying, "It's all right. I love you. It's all right."

I wonder, she thought, *if this will happen to me.*

She saw him through a series of bad chest colds—in spite of the fact that nobody would bring her the requested goose grease to rub on his chest. In fact, they wouldn't even let her make him an onion plaster. They could have done that easily enough; there were plenty of onions in the kitchen.

She nursed him through a fingerful of warts that bothered him a great deal. The young doctors around the nursing home hadn't learned about using castor oil on warts. Louisa talked Wallace into bringing her some anyway, and the warts went away.

There came a time for Chris when nobody could see him through anymore illnesses.

It began with another of the chest colds. This one worsened into pneumonia. Chris couldn't struggle out of bed and there was a tube in his nostrils, another in his arm.

In all of their fifty years together, Louisa had never seen him lie so still or look so pale and weak.

"My dear," he mouthed, almost too feeble for even the faintest whisper. "It's time to go home, and I believe I'll go before you." His eyes closed, and for one wild, panic-stricken moment, Louisa thought that Chris had left her.

"No!" Her whisper was almost a shout.

His eyes opened again, and he shook his head. "Not yet," he said. "Not yet."

When Louisa first realized how ill Chris was, she prayed great prayers of longing, pleading for his life, begging God to give him extra years . . . or months . . . or days . . . or even hours. The future seemed barren and meaningless without him.

One morning again she awoke and forgot that she was old. Lying there beneath the warm comfort of her blankets, she thought that she was young and would soon leap from the bed to face a strenuous day.

There was no mirror for her to look into, and she kept on thinking so until she turned to look at Chris. The sight of him brought the fact of his age—and her own—painfully back to her.

Chris lay in bed, shriveled and gray—the gray of the hovering clouds that threatened snow outside the window—dying, yet clinging to life as if he knew beyond knowing how she dreaded his leaving.

It was then, with tears, that she asked the Lord to release him. "I've been wrong, dear Friend," she said, "to try to hold Chris here with me. He needs to go with you. He needs to go home."

Was it only coincidence that only a few hours later, a nurse taking his pulse turned softly to Louisa? "He's gone dear."

And now, thought Louisa—reaching toward him, blinded with tears, as if to say, *Wait . . . don't go without me—I am alone.*

Alone. The word wrapped itself around her, filling the deep places of her soul. For one awful moment she felt as if the whole world had died, and she alone were left. Her terrible loneliness emptied her of all feeling. Even when other people came into the room, she hardly recognized them as persons like herself. The only one who really had liked her and cared about her and understood her was gone from her. He would never come back.

Outside, the hovering clouds gave up their burden at last; soft flakes began to sift down to cover the ground, tiny messengers heralding the end of autumn and the beginning of winter.

A horrible thought came to Louisa then: *Nobody needs me anymore. It was so nice to be needed, but now nobody does.*

She sat there, waiting for them to come and get that part of her husband he had left behind when his spirit went on to a better life.

She was not left to wait alone. The residents of Parmenter County Home who were able to know and understand that death had occurred came to her, to share in her grief for a brief moment.

Jessie came—softly, for once without words. She held Louisa's hand and cried for her.

"I didn't take good enough care of him, I guess," Louisa told her. "I feel awful bad about that. He was mine . . . and I didn't take good enough care of him."

She said the words and sank back into the bed.

It was not until Chris's funeral service that she began to come out of her depression. The old words Louisa had heard so many times at so many other funerals were spoken again. "But I would not have you to be ignorant, brethren, concerning them which are asleep, that ye sorrow not, even as others which have no hope."

"Yes," Louisa whispered, grabbing on to the words of scripture like a drowning woman clinging to a life preserver. "Oh, yes. There *is* hope. He cannot come back to me. But it is well with him. And I shall soon go to him."

After Chris's death, though, Louisa's mind did not seem to work quite as well as it had. It seemed as if it had slipped into a lower gear.

10

A LOWER GEAR

Occasionally real confusion filled Louisa's mind. When that happened, it took time and effort to straighten everything out again.

Her bad days came more and more frequently.

Sometimes she woke expecting to be home with the wedding ring quilt and Chris in the bed across the room. On those days she had to work her way back through the years to reality.

There were days when she couldn't quite bring herself back.

On one occasion there were many visitors who filled her room. Was it a party of some kind? She spent the entire time trying to understand who they were and why they sang "Happy Birthday."

She grieved over them, mourning her loss of memory as face after face bent in front of her, filled with love and concern, trying to communicate something to her.

The hum of voices in the small room was loud, and all of the bending-over-her people seemed to mumble. It was like a television set with the sound turned too low: faces mouthing words that flew into the air before her ears could reach out and gather them in.

When the party was over, they all smiled and hugged, patted and kissed, and said good-by.

Louisa smiled back and waved, hoping they were all happy, and that they would never know how far beyond her the occasion had been.

Wallace and Mary came to take her to the funeral of an old friend. She did well during the service. The name of the friend, repeated, kept her aware.

But at the cemetery, she could not remember why they were there.

For one horrifying moment, seeing relatives and friends gathered around her, she thought, *Why . . . it's me!*

Looking down, she knew she was wrong. She could still manage to flex the stiffened fingers that hung at arm's length. Her tired legs in their heavy stockings still stood upright.

They weren't gathered for Louisa B. For whom then?

She never remembered.

Yet, in spite of the bad days, there was a power that sustained her, a power that kept her whole most of the time while all around her others tottered into senility: Louisa *knew.*

She knew whom she trusted. She knew in whom she believed. She knew to whose family she belonged. She even knew how her own story was going to end.

Over and over, Louisa read favorite verses in the dog-eared Bible, holding the magnifying glass above the small print. "In whom ye also trusted, after that ye heard the word of truth, the gospel of your salvation: in whom also after that ye believed, ye were sealed with that holy Spirit of promise, which is the earnest of our inheritance until the redemption of the purchased possession, unto the praise of his glory."

Knowing that—knowing God—made all the difference as far as Louisa was concerned.

She talked with God often.

Sometimes she grumbled. They had been friends for a long time, after all. If a person couldn't grumble to her best Friend, to whom could she grumble?

At other times she just went over in her mind all of the years that they had been through together. "Jesus, blessed Jesus," she would begin. "My loving Savior. You are my Lord and my Redeemer. The Author and Finisher of my life and my faith. My life has been hid in you alone. The road was rough many times, but the sun shone through the dark clouds. You and me, Lord, we travelled it together. Thank you, Lord."

She wrote it down once, just like that, so the others would have it after she was gone and know how it had been between them.

She never asked for much. After the first days when she had asked God to let her go home and she had learned that it was not going to happen, she decided that the rest home must somehow be his will for her, and she stopped bothering him about it.

After that, she went about the business of being old Louisa just as she had gone about the business of being young Louisa, hand-in-hand with her beloved Lord and Savior.

"I can do all things," she would remind herself, "through Christ, who strengtheneth me . . . and that includes growing old."

She became so close to him in those last years of her life that people who knew her said all you had to do was to get close to Louisa and you wanted to kneel and worship Louisa's God.

Life still was not perfect. Louisa was 106 years old when she died. She had had a lot of years to live with being old. But while she wept over the problems of aging, she never wept alone. She wept with a hand on her shoulder, and Another's tears mingled with her own.

Nevertheless, she did weep. Even a godly old woman never quite gets over wanting to go home.

Living at Parmenter County while that longing raged within her was only one of the adjustments she had to make as age took a tighter and tighter grip on her body, mind, and soul. The worst of those adjustments was to remember that Chris was gone.

Gayle, Wallace's son-in-law, came to see her a few days after the funeral and brought some fresh green onions. Louisa's first thought was, *Oh, Chris, look what he's brought us!*

Eating them was bittersweet. She enjoyed the fresh crispness with her meals. But with every bite she could imagine Chris's pleasure if he had been there to share them. The tears in her eyes as she ate did not come from the sting of onions.

Some of the things she needed to face those last years of life were already well learned:

Take smaller steps than you used to, Louisa, she had taught herself. Walking was safer that way.

If you have to step off a curb somewhere, do it sideways, rather than head on.

If someone took her out at night, she always clung to the younger arm. The light of moon, stars, and street lights was not enough for someone her age to see in the dark.

The accidents she had had were often caused by changing position too quickly, so she had learned to stand slowly, to wait quietly for a second or two before she moved after standing, and to be sure of her balance before she took a step. She needed to remember all of that even when she used a walker.

The staff of Parmenter County had insisted she not get up in the night and move around in the dark—not even in the familiar surroundings of her own room. They were right because she knew that she needed to take time after waking to get her sense of direction adjusted. She knew it, but that didn't mean she liked it. Once in a while, when they were too slow getting to her, she would get up and move anyhow, just to prove she could do it. If she were very careful, it worked out all right.

But if she weren't . . . . She tripped and fell once on such a night. Shuffling along in the near-dark, the only light in the room came from the glow of the ceiling fixtures in the hall outside. A shuffle works fine when the way is clear, but it wasn't. She shuffled right into a shoe that she had not tucked far enough under the bed, and she fell.

After that she remembered that she needed to lift her feet when she walked.

Old Louisa learned to hold a glass differently from the way young Louisa had done it. Instead of wrapping her hand around it, she put her little finger on the bottom, so the glass couldn't slip so easily from her fingers. Sometimes, when she seemed very shaky, she would use two hands, like a small child with the first cup of milk.

After Chris's death and the beginning of serious memory lapses, Louisa learned to keep a notepad and pencil close at hand to jot down things that she was afraid of forgetting.

That kept her out of trouble at times—when Wallace and Mary came she always tried to remember to write down, "Wallace and Mary were here today," and the date.

She wrote down her feelings, too, and once or twice that got her *into* trouble.

There was the time she wrote a whole page about Wallace and Mary. "Sometimes," said the trembling letters scrawled across the unlined paper, "I'm afraid I don't like Wallace very much anymore. He doesn't treat me like a person. He acts as if I can't think for myself. He and Mary make all the decisions, and they make me stay here where I hate it. Oh, dear God . . . help me to love my son again."

When Louisa wrote that, she sat and looked at it, and she was a little ashamed of having written it. She was going to tear it out and throw it away, but there was a little bit that was good at the top of the page—some other things she wanted to remember—and she couldn't throw that away, too.

"I'll recopy the good," she decided, "and throw away the bad."

She didn't do it at the time, and she forgot, until Mary came.

It was a serious argument—if you could call it an argument when only one person talked. It was more a bawling out of Louisa.

"What *is this,* Mother?" demanded Mary as she straightened Louisa's nightstand. "What does it mean you don't like Wallace anymore?" A thin, white anger line formed around her mouth while her eyes flashed anger and pain.

Oh dear, thought Louisa, *I did a bad thing.*

"I suppose it means you don't like *me,* either! Well, let me tell you . . . !" An exasperated sigh escaped Mary, as she left the sentence unfinished.

"I just don't understand you, Mother!" She shouted and turned toward the door. She stopped to say it again softly, but somehow more fiercely than the shout had been, "I don't understand you at *all!*"

No, thought Louisa, *I don't imagine you do. Nobody understands old age until they've been there—and then it's really too late to do much about it.*

That's how it was with a lot of life. Nobody could understand how it was about experiences until they had lived through them.

Louisa couldn't understand how her mother had felt about Papa walking out on her . . . until Amos had walked out.

She hadn't understood how a woman could ever leave her husband to get a divorce—until that day when she knew finally she was going to have to divorce Amos.

Even the most important thing in her life—her faith—was something Louisa had not understood until she was sixteen years old.

Before that, she *thought* she understood, but the reality of a faith experience had escaped her.

It wasn't that she didn't want to understand. From the time she was old enough to remember, Louisa had made the weekly Sunday morning pilgrimage to church. In the "Defenseless Mennonite" Church near Pandora she had learned to sing the old songs before she could read: *Nun Danket Alle Gott* and *Die Gnade Uns're Herr Jesu Christi*. She had learned to sit quietly during the long, dull sermons and nibble on a cracker or play with a handkerchief. Mama knew how to turn a handkerchief into all kinds of playthings to keep a little girl quiet: a mouse, a pig, or two babies wrapped up in a blanket.

When Louisa was older, they gave her a Bible, which she was expected to carry with her every week. She was also expected to listen to the sermons. They were still long and usually dull. The Elder's voice was so solemn that it made Louisa sleepy. She learned to sit up straight and look as if she were paying attention while she daydreamed to escape the boredom.

The fundamentals of her faith were learned there, though.

A Defenseless Mennonite was expected to live at peace with everyone, to trust God in all situations, to love and help one's neighbors, to honor one's parents. Louisa had some trouble with that last one because her Papa ran off so much of the time. But he came back—repentant and asking forgiveness of friends and family—as often as he went. Everyone else forgave him and Louisa tried to as well.

And although dress restrictions were later discarded, in those days, Defenseless Mennonites were expected to dress in very plain clothes, according to traditions established by the church. The women wore dark dresses with bonnets and shawls.

Louisa obeyed the rules of her church because it was expected of her. It wasn't until she was sixteen that she understood that there was something more to faith than that.

She came home from a neighboring farm late one afternoon where she had been doing day work to find the little children crying. Papa had left home again.

Mama was not crying, though. She was holding Bertha and running her fingers along the twists of the child's silken braids. She was singing softly, first to one child, then to another.

Louisa shed no tears, either. Instead, she comforted the other children and busied herself with finding temporary homes where they could work for their keep. But an angry bitterness raged inside her.

What kind of man would . . . ?

It was then that Louisa realized there was a difference between her mother's faith and her own. Louisa could do all the right things outside but inside her, there was turmoil.

Her mother's faith was deep and took care of the turmoil.

"God in heaven," Louisa prayed. "What is this? What is wrong with me? Are you there? Will you help me?"

Louisa cried out to her Creator. And when at last she was ready to listen, there was a voice ready to answer.

"I'm right here," the voice spoke in silence to the deep places of her soul. "I've been waiting for you to want me."

"You have?" Louisa asked.

"Yes," the voice replied. "You have been trying to live on other people's faith. You need to learn for yourself that I love you and that you can depend on me."

The voice was gentle and kind and seemed, somehow, to be filled with tears as though weeping for her, although she could not weep for herself.

Almost as quickly as that, it was done. Louisa knew the power of God's presence. She knew that a person could devote a lifetime to serving and worshiping this One, and never tire.

"I'm yours," she said. "My life is yours. Please take it and do whatever you want with me." Shortly afterwards, Louisa was baptized and joined the Defenseless Mennonite Church.

Although there were many difficult days ahead for her, she had found assurance in a life of peace.

Ninety years later, Louisa Basinger sat, old and tired and lonely for her daughter whose feelings she had wounded so deeply, and knew that her commitment to God had been right. She had given her life into his keeping, and she had never tired of him.

Mary forgave her after a while, of course. She always did. This time she even said, "I'm sorry, Mama. I shouldn't have hollered at you. I don't know why I get so upset over little things like that. I ought to know better."

"It's all right," said Louisa patting her daughter's hand.

It was a nice day, a good day for making peace with somebody she loved. The sun was shining, warm, but not too hot, while all outdoors showed signs of spring. Louisa looked forward to a drive in the countryside with Mary and Wallace. When Wallace arrived, Mary decided not to tell him about the note she had found.

It felt good to see all the familiar places again. They drove over to Pandora and out by Riley Creek, to where the old wooden covered bridge used to be. The new metal one wasn't nearly so pretty, but the creek was nice.

They drove down one country road after another, and Louisa savored the sights and sounds of spring—hopping robins, tree branches bursting with new buds, and the roar of a tractor at work on spring plowing—held them close to her and tried to cry quietly to escape her children's notice.

Wallace might even have driven past the house on Monroe Street, but when Louisa thought he was headed in that direction, she whispered softly with a catch in her voice, "No, please,

Wallace. Don't go there. I don't think I could stand to see it—and not be able to stay."

He turned, instead, and headed out of town. After several miles of silence they drove up behind a young Amish man and his wife, riding close together in a buggy, behind a stylish bay mare. Wallace passed carefully to the left as Mary commented that they were probably newlyweds.

Louisa traveled a lot farther than Wallace and Mary did that day. The sight of the buggy and the young couple sent her down a long path of memory, to eighty years and more in the past, to another young marriage, one that started out to be a fine union.

People write books about marriages that started out like that—young couples, very much in love, facing incredible odds while they tried to carve a home and a family out of the hard rock life handed them.

And so while Wallace and Mary drove the quiet back roads of rural Ohio, Louisa traveled down her own road to the past. While they talked to each other in the front seat about the Amish and their Mennonite ancestors, Louisa sat in the back seat and talked to Mama and Amos and her children and sat for a while in the old log cabin, rocking one of her babies. She sat in the frame house for a while too. Then she pushed the baby in the buggy to Pandora to visit her parents.

It was a very long trip for a single afternoon.

Louisa was back in her room at Parmenter County Home physically much sooner than she was back mentally. It was one of those times when it was very difficult to return to the present.

"Thank you, Amos," she said to Wallace when he helped her to her room.

And, "Don't worry, Mama," she said to Mary, when Mary hugged her good-by. "It'll be all right."

Wallace and Mary both sighed as they left her. It was the last time they took her out of the nursing home.

11

ROOMMATES

The years were ticked off by the hands of the clock in the hall as Louisa's life wound down.

Though she was surrounded by people, she was lonely. Nobody, it seemed, was able to be quite what she wanted him or her to be.

For a while there were some people who came to hold church services in the home. Somehow nothing seemed right about it. The hymns were an uninspiring wail, accompanied by a tiny electric organ which produced a grating whine that was most unpleasant, even to Louisa's faded hearing. Although the preacher was young, his voice was a drone that said nothing at all to an old woman whose ears could not separate one word from another.

Sometimes when those folks came, Louisa would sit with her eyes closed and try to imagine herself back in the precious old Missionary Church in Pandora where she and Chris attended. It never quite worked. She would open her eyes again to a greater loneliness than before.

The staff at the home, for the most part, treated Louisa as a job rather than as a person and their friend. It was their business to be jolly and friendly and to take good care of her. It was their business, also, to remember that she was over a hundred years old, which made her something of a celebrity.

She liked most of them, and most of them—she thought—liked her. But it's hard to get really close to a job in a heart-to-heart way, so most of the staff missed what really learning to know Louisa might have meant to them. And Louisa missed getting to know them.

Visiting strangers who brought church or entertainment were one story. Attendants were another. Residents were still another.

Louisa thought the other residents almost completely impossible. She moved among them, but in some strange way she was never quite one of them in her own eyes.

Under the circumstances, her relatives and friends from outside the nursing home were the natural people for her to center her life on. Yet that didn't quite work out, either.

Wallace and Mary or others would come to see her, and always there were things Louisa needed them to know.

"I've been so tired lately," she would say. "I miss the out-of-doors . . . . I wish I could go home . . . . There's hardly anyone here I can talk to . . . . I can't remember things the way I used to . . . . I don't like the food . . . . They're starting to talk about keeping me in a wheelchair instead of letting me use the walker."

The visitors would stay as long as they could. On leaving, they would shake their heads and mutter to themselves.

"You didn't stay long," Louisa would call after them. "Come sooner next time and stay longer."

After one such visit, Jessie rolled through Louisa's door. "Well, dear," she said. "I see you've had some company." She picked up the purple elephant from Louisa's windowsill and took it into her lap to straighten its necktie and its ears. Louisa watched her carefully.

"Yes," said Louisa. "That was my Mama and Papa."

Jessie stopped still and looked at her. It was a careful, cautioning look. Louisa caught it and held it for a moment, then spoke again. "No," she said. "That wasn't Mama and Papa at all. That was my son, Wallace, and my daughter, Mary." She smiled shyly, pleased with herself.

"I can do it," she said. "When I really try, I can keep things straight."

"You're right," said Jessie. "You can." Again she sat and looked at Louisa, considering whether what she was thinking should be said.

Apparently she decided it should, "There's a thing I've got to tell you, Mrs. B., about that Wallace, and that Mary—and some others," she said.

"They are starting to go away from you muttering."

"Muttering?" said Louisa. "How muttering?"

"When they leave, they are always saying things." It was difficult for Jessie to explain without hurting her.

"What things?" Louisa's voice had taken on just a touch of impatience.

"Things like . . . they don't like to come anymore, because all you do is complain."

"Oh," said Louisa, and that was all. What more could she say when the pain of the accusation shot through her heart and closed her mouth?

Jessie came to Louisa then—"Damn!" she said, coming. "I've hurt your feelings!"—wheeling across the room to take her hand and hold it, comforting.

Louisa was so occupied with the new, uncomfortable truth that she didn't even notice Jessie's profanity. In the quiet moments of comforting, she vowed that she would stop grumbling—that she would never give Jessie or anyone else a chance to say a thing like that about her again.

But when they came again to see her, Louisa found the vow hard to keep. How do you engage in idle, happy chit-chat with someone who thinks everything is fine for you? How do you keep from telling that person how bad everything is when they can't seem to see it for themselves?

In her last years, Louisa continued to grumble, and the grumbling was a wedge that drove itself deeper between herself and the persons she most wanted to have close to her. One of the things she complained about the most was roommates.

It was in the nature of life in a nursing home that Louisa would have to have a roommate. With Chris gone—the pain of his death still made her heart ache every time she looked at the smooth spread over the empty bed—it made sense that Louisa should not occupy it alone.

"How about Jessie Henderson?" Louisa asked when they first mentioned it to her. "She's a nice woman. And we do seem to get along together fairly well."

But they argued aginst her suggestion. "No, Mrs. B. You don't want *her* in here. You want someone more like yourself . . . someone your own age."

They began to come, a series of unspoken comments on what the world of younger, working people around her thought of Louisa. Some of the roommates moved to another room in a few days or a few weeks, complaining that Louisa was too hard to live with. There were some who died, right there in the room with her, silent reminders that there would be for Louisa, too, a day of release. Others just vegetated, as if they were without the courage or strength to die.

One of them even read Louisa's mail.

The first roommate was Sarah.

"Good morning, Mrs. B.," sang an aide. "This is Sarah." That was the first announcement Louisa had of the woman's coming.

Ancient and bedfast, her face was so wrinkled that she reminded Louisa of a cartoon—the kind you look at one way to see a person smiling and turned upside-down, it's a person frowning.

The aide placed her in Chris's bed. *I don't like that,* thought Louisa. *Someone else in my dear husband's bed. I don't like that at all!* But there was nothing she could do about it.

Sarah was a moaner. The moment she was put into the bed, she began the soft, whimpering moan that was to last until the day she died.

"Ohhhhhhhh, deeeeear," she said. "Ohhhhhhhh. Ohhhhhhhh, dear!"

"What's the matter?" asked Louisa from her wheelchair.

"Ohhhhhhhhhhhhh, dear."

"What's the *matter?*"

"The paaaaaaain," moaned Sarah. "Ohhhhhhhh, deeeeeear."

"Do you need a nurse?" asked Louisa. "You can call one by pushing the button on your night stand."

"Ohhhhhhhh, Deeeeeear."

"Do you want me to call a nurse for you?"

"Ohhhhhhh, deeeeeear."

Louisa reached for the button.

The nurse, for once, came quickly. Frowning, she popped her head through the door, looked at the two of them, and said, "Well?"

"Ohhhhhhhhhh, deeeeeear," said Louisa's roommate.

Louisa nodded toward the other bed. "I think there's something the matter with her."

The nurse shrugged her shoulders sighing heavily, and rolled her eyes toward the ceiling. "Mrs. B.," she said, her lips stiff. "Mrs. B., the only thing wrong with that woman is that she wants attention. She's not getting it, so she makes a fuss."

"Please," she said, "*please* don't call us again. We'll take care of Sarah." And she was gone.

Louisa felt as if a wall had gone up between herself and the nurse, and between herself and her roommate as well. It was as if she were banging her head against the wall in a desperate, futile attempt to make some sense out of it all.

People who groan like that are in pain. Sarah was groaning; therefore, she must be in pain.

Nobody seemed to agree with her.

The nurses obviously didn't.

When Sarah's family came to visit, Louisa asked them about the groaning.

"Don't worry," they said. "She's been doing that for years."

Sarah herself, when Louisa asked if she needed a doctor, seemed to have the same opinion as the others. "What's the use of having a doctor?" she said. "When I have a doctor, he just says, 'Oh, Sarah, what do you expect? After all, you're not getting any younger.' No, I don't need a doctor." Sarah quietly went back to her groaning.

The moans didn't bother Louisa much during the daytime. She was still mobile, even though the aides strapped her into a wheelchair and made her stay there. She could leave the room whenever she wanted to get away from that perpetual soft wail.

Nights were another story. Louisa lay awake for several nights before she finally found a solution.

That first night, Louisa asked politely, over and over, "Would you be real quiet, please?"

Sarah, depending on her mental condition at the moment, would answer either, "Of course, dearie"—or "Ohhhhhh, deeeeeear!"

It went on like that most of the night, until Sarah dropped into a light slumber and Louisa was able to get a little rest.

The next night began the same way. After a couple of hours of sleeplessness, Louisa decided to call in reinforcements, and reached for the buzzer.

The nurse who came in answer was a gentle woman, loving and compassionate. Louisa was glad to see her.

"I can't get to sleep," said Louisa. "And I'm awfully tired." She gestured toward the other bed, where a low, "Ohhhhh, deeeeear," interrupted her. "Do you think you could get her to be quiet?"

"I'll try," the nurse replied, and crossed the room. "Sarah," said the nurse, "are you awake?"

Now that, thought Louisa, *is a dumb question!*

"Sarah, your roommate is having a hard time getting to sleep. Do you think you could be real quiet for a while?"

"Uh-huh," said Sarah. "I surely could." Louisa could see her head bobbing against the pillow as she nodded.

"There," said the nurse. She smiled at Louisa as she passed. "I think that will do it." She left the room.

"Ohhhhhhh, deeeeear," said Sarah.

"Oh, dear," said Louisa.

As lights went out on the third night, Louisa felt a sense of desperation flowing restlessly through her. *I need some sleep,* she thought. *Is every night going to be like this for the rest of my life?"*

"Ohhhhhhhh, deeeear," from her roommate.

"Shhhhhhhh!" hissed Louisa into the darkness between them.

"Ohhhhhhhh, deeeeear," replied the roommate.

"Shhhhhhh!" said Louisa again.

None of it did any good. They exchanged "oh, dears" and "shhhhhh's" most of the night. Toward morning Louisa woke, tired, but grateful to realize that she had finally slept a little.

I have to think of some way to deal with this, she said to herself. Weariness and anger filled her. When an aide came to help her dress, Louisa wanted nothing but to stay in bed.

But what good would it do? she thought.

She was out of bed and dressed before she began talking to the aide about it. "That old woman in the other bed," she said, "keeps me awake all night with her groaning. Do you know if there's any way I could get a different roommate?"

There wasn't. Louisa explored all of the avenues she knew. The aide didn't know about things like that. One nurse didn't answer at all, just snorted. Another explained politely that such things just weren't done. Sarah would stay there. A counselor told her that he would do everything he could to help the two of them adjust, but move?—no, it was impossible.

The fourth night began as usual. It didn't *begin,* really. It just continued the way it had been all day and for several days before that.

"Ohhhhhhh, deeeeear!"

"Please, Sarah, be quiet tonight and let me sleep."

"Ohhhhhhh, deeeeeeear!"

Pshaw! thought Louisa. *She's just like a spoiled child. It doesn't matter what anybody says, she just goes ahead and does what she wants. Just like a spoiled child!*

That was when the idea came. If Sarah acted like a spoiled child, why not treat her like one?

Louisa propped herself on one elbow and looked toward the other bed. "Sarah," she said, loudly and firmly. "Sarah . . . you be quiet *right now* . . . or I'm going to *spank your bottom!*"

"Oh, *dear!*" said Sarah.

The room was filled with a glorious silence. Louisa fell quickly into the comfortable, rewarding sleep of a woman who has met a challenge—and won. *Just like a spoiled child,* was her last thought.

That wasn't the end of the problem forever, of course. Sarah periodically fell back into her old habit. But Louisa knew how to handle the situation, and it never defeated her again.

Sarah died not long afterwards. Strangely, the flame of life that had burned so noisily toward the end, flickered and went out with only a whisper. Louisa woke one morning to find an aide bending over Sarah, trying to wake her—she never woke again.

Louisa was somewhat uncomfortable with the suddenness of Sarah's death, but she had seen a lot of dying over the years, and it seemed so natural that it didn't bother her for long.

A few days later, they brought Mrs. Creasel to her.

Mrs. Creasel didn't stay long. She was new to rest home living—how well Louisa could remember what that was like—and she didn't adjust well. She cried a lot and was very emotional about almost everything that happened. The staff couldn't even give her a pill without provoking an emotional outburst.

Mrs. Creasel refused to eat unless someone from her family came to feed her.

After a few weeks, her family decided they could cope better in familiar surroundings and took her home.

Cynthia, who lived in the past, was next. Over and over she told Louisa the same stories, until even Louisa, whose memory wasn't what it had been, remembered that she had heard them all before and grew tired of it all. That didn't stop Cynthia.

After that, there was Bethy . . . and the cat.

Bethy came from a family that was too busy to care for her, so they put her in the nursing home. Nobody knew where the cat came from.

It appeared in the doorway not long after Bethy did, and Bethy adopted it. When an aide, a nurse, or somebody else in authority would notice the cat, it would be thrown out. It always came back.

Bethy fed it, petted it, and let it sleep on her lap—beneath a towel or a pillow case or an old gray sweater so that it couldn't be seen and evicted.

The amusing thing was that although the cat remembered Bethy and came back to her every time someone threw it out, Bethy never quite remembered the cat.

Each time it strolled through the door, tail high, haughtily surveying the room, Bethy was surprised.

"Why, look," she would say. "Here's a little pussy cat, come to see us. Here, kitty, kitty, kitty."

"Kitty" would come. Bethy would hide it on her lap, as if she had just thought of the idea for the first time.

"See," she would say, if she found a visitor who could be trusted. "See what I've got." And she would lift a corner of the towel or whatever she had chosen to hide it to disclose gleaming black eyes and a set of twitching whiskers.

The cat was a handy thing for Bethy to have around. It seemed, somehow, to increase her value in her own eyes. "Well," she might say, "there doesn't seem to be much I'm good for anymore." Her voice carried a hint of the peculiar nostalgia that belongs to those who have always been workers—until forced by old age to become loafers. "But at least I can feed the cat."

Feed it she did.

At mealtime, Bethy would take one of the bowls from her tray to put on the floor for "kitty." Often, as she reached down with it, the bowl would rock out of control, and the contents would end up—all or partly—on the floor. "Oooops!" Bethy would say. "I seem to have spilled a dab, here. Could you wipe it up for me?"

"No," Louisa always answered, unable to keep the irritation out of her voice. Why *couldn't* that woman remember that she, Louisa, wasn't hired help. "I can't reach it either. You'll have to wait for one of the aides."

Some days Bethy would have had quite a collection of spills before an aide came—except that the cat did a fair job of cleaning up.

It was handy in another way, too.

Louisa didn't like to think about it, let alone live in the same room with Bethy and the problem. But a roommate—at Parmenter County—was a roommate until death or the administration changed it. There was nothing she could do about it.

It was, she supposed, a matter of Bethy's having been raised in a rural home where family members kept a chamber pot by their bed at night, so they wouldn't have to struggle all the way to the outhouse in the dark and cold if it were necessary to relieve themselves.

Louisa understood that. She had been raised in such a house herself.

But there surely must have been a time in Bethy's life when she no longer had to use a pot at night. Yet now in her senility, she seemed to miss the pot.

There were many nights when Louisa could hear Bethy fumbling her way out of bed. Next would come silence while the other woman reached out into the darkness, looking for what was not there.

Finally in the midst of the fumbling would come a metallic clunk, as Bethy's groping hand found the waste basket.

In the morning, the first aide who came into the room would groan, "Oh, *Bethy!* Not again!"

Bethy would look up, innocent and unknowing.

"Look at this wastebasket. Just look at it!" the aide would say—or something worse.

When Bethy looked was when the cat became most useful. About that time, he would stir and stretch himself and ease his way out of whatever wrinkle in the bedspread he had spent the night in.

"That damn cat!" Bethy would say every morning, looking. "That damn cat! Just look what he did in my waste basket. Phew!"

Ugh! Louisa would say inside herself. *Ugh! How can she stand to do that?—and then* lie *about it!"*

"Well," said Jessie on a morning when she had stopped by in time to catch Bethy's act and Louisa's comment, "I suppose

she doesn't really know she does it. I mean . . . I suppose she
knows at the time, but by morning . . . you know how Bethy is.
She probably doesn't remember a thing. She probably believes
the cat really did it."

"Maybe," said Louisa, the closest she could come to admit-
ting that Bethy's habits might not be disgusting on purpose.

Jessie straightened a couple of the pictures on Louisa's
dresser as she asked, "Want to come down to my room for your
breakfast? To get away from the smell?"

"Thank you," said Louisa. "I believe I would." She turned to
look at Jessie for the first time since the younger woman had
entered room 34.

"Dear God in heaven!" exploded Louisa. "What happened
to *you?*"

Jessie's face was bruised and swollen. A lopsided bandage
sat over one ear and wound around her head. Her wheelchair
was new.

"My chair and I had a little accident—with a car."

"You were in a wreck?"

"Well, the car hit me when I was out for a walk," she hesitated and corrected herself, "for a *roll* a couple of days
ago."

Louisa shook her head. "You should be more careful." She
leaned toward Jessie to examine the injuries as well as she
could with eyes that were nearly worn out.

"Woman," said Louisa, "you must have been trying to get
yourself killed."

At that, Jessie smiled softly and led the way down the hall
to her room and breakfast.

It was good; it was always good to spend time with someone whose mind was clear and sharp. In her outward
appearance, Jessie was declining, resembling the other
residents more and more. Inwardly, she was still quite a
woman.

There wasn't as much conversation between them as
there once had been. Now it was Jessie who talked most. Louisa
was better at listening than at talking some days, anyway, and
what Jessie had to say was so often deep with thought.

"I don't understand," said Jessie over their cold tea and limp toast, "why it is that they treat old age like some kind of disease? Being born and growing old are both natural things, but folks treat them like diseases. Life starts out in a hospital . . . and it ends up in the same place. Foolish, that's what I call it."

Louisa considered Bethy and wasn't so sure. But it was an interesting thought.

The only bad thing about a good conversation with Jessie was that sooner or later it ended, and Louisa had to go back to room 34 and Bethy—or someone like her.

After Bethy it was Angie, a three-year-old mind in an eighty-nine-year-old body.

Angie tattled. *"She,"* she would say, pointing a bony, accusing finger in the general direction of Louisa, "didn't eat her green beans."

"*She* was talking about going home again. She's not supposed to do that."

"*She* wrote something on a piece of paper and put it in her drawer."

"*She* and her friend were talking about me."

Angie never closed the bathroom door when she used the stool. Whenever Angie headed for the toilet, Louisa would worry that one of her relatives or friends would come to visit and find the old woman enthroned in the tiny room. Somehow the complete lack of dignity she observed in Angie seemed to taint Louisa as well.

The three-year-old in Angie loved to correct the people around her. "Don't leave the pillow on top of your spread in the morning," she would say. "Don't leave any milk in your glass. Don't walk to the door; get into your wheelchair."

If Louisa ever corrected her—"You aren't supposed to leave your dirty clothes under your bed."—Angie's temper would flare.

"Too bad I'm not!" she would reply, and do it her own way anyhow.

It was hard for Louisa to live with that, but there were other times that had been harder.

Before long, Angie, too, was gone.

The woman who read Louisa's mail replaced her.

Louisa could not believe it. She was accustomed, of course, to the fact that she could no longer read letters for herself. Someone else—a nurse or a visitor—had to do it. But it was always, until Tib moved in, her own choice as to who would do the reading. That Tib dared to make it otherwise left a raw wound on Louisa's soul. She almost cried whenever she saw Tib with one of her letters.

The first time it happened, Louisa came wheeling down the hall from the day room to turn in to room 34. Tib, she saw, had mail.

"Hello," said Louisa. "I'm back."

There was no answer. "I see the mail is here," said Louisa. "Was there any for me?"

"Just a minute," said Tib, and went on with her reading.

Louisa waited patiently for the other to finish. "Is there any mail for me?" she asked again.

"Sure," said Tib, and held out the opened, rumpled letter with its envelope.

"No," said Louisa, impatient now. "That's yours. Is there any for *me?*"

"I told you *yes,*" said Tib testily. "And this is it." She held it out again. "Do you want it or not?"

Louisa took the papers, unbelieving, dropped them into her lap, and scooted out the door to find better eyes.

"Excuse me," she said to an aide. "Is this letter for me?"

The aide glanced down. "Yup," she said, patting Louisa on the shoulder. "Want me to read it to you?"

Louisa felt as if she had touched an electric fence. The shock kept her wordless. The aide shrugged her shoulders and went down the hall without reading the letter.

"Well, I swan," said Louisa, watching the pale blue dress disappear into the mist that was all her eyes could see. "I swan!"

Louisa guarded her mail more carefully after that incident. Most of it came to her unread, but still Tib got some letters.

"Listen to this," Tib said from the other bed one day at nap time. She held up a piece of lined notebook paper and began to read.

" 'Dear Gramma,' it says. 'How are you doing these days?' and then there is a bunch of other stuff. But listen to this. This is the important thing: 'Carl and I are getting a divorce.' "

"Who's Carl?" asked the roommate. And then, flipping to the end of the letter, "Who's Grace?"

"Oh, my," said Louisa. "Oh, my." Her voice rose painfully, then faded into tears. "That's my letter again, isn't it? How long have you had it? Grace is my great-granddaughter. Carl is her husband."

There was suddenly no more to say. Louisa struggled up from the bed, hobbled across the room by carefully holding to furniture, and took the letter in her trembling fingers.

She felt bad, of course, that Tib had got her mail again. God only knew how long she had had the letter before she shared it with Louisa. But Grace . . . and Carl . . . and the *divorce*. Oh, dear God, the news tore at her very soul.

Because she knew—oh, how well she knew—what divorce meant, and the agony of it, and the destruction and death that hung in the air before birth and new life could come out of the broken family.

"Dear God," prayed Louisa then. "Please make it all right for them. Make their family all of a piece again.

"But if you can't . . . ," she started to say, then emended it, " . . . if you don't, deal gently with them. Don't let it be as hard for them as it was for me."

After all those years, she could still remember the dreams and the despair they left behind when she woke.

"Oh, my dear, sweet Jesus," she prayed, then. "Let my Grace and her Carl have better dreams than that."

Maybe we could all use a little something good in the way of dreams.

Then, into Louisa's life came Johnny.

12

JOHNNY

Johnny, who loved Louisa and cared for her as if she were his own. Johnny, who treated her like a whole person again. Johnny, who left to save himself, and in the saving of himself nearly destroyed Louisa.

The first time she saw him she had no warning of the closeness that would one day spring up between them.

Johnny wrestled a breakfast cart through the door and said, "Good morning, ladies. My name is Johnny."

Louisa looked up, startled by his appearance. His nose was too long; his eyes were dark and deep set; and his long hair was tied back in a pony tail.

Young men in pony tails! thought Louisa. *What is this world coming to?*

Johnny smiled and his dark eyes were alive with a glow that told her that he cared.

He may not have been handsome but the smile and his caring made Louisa feel good.

A few weeks later when Johnny brought her some fresh green onions to go with her lunch, Louisa forgave him the long hair.

Johnny was a young man to whom small things were important—small things like seeing to it that Tib didn't get any more of Louisa's mail. These small things did something big for the old woman, as well as for others living in the nursing home. The message he sent them was that life was for living—and living could be done well even in a place like Parmenter County.

For Louisa, it started with birds.

"Look, Mrs. B.," said Johnny. "There's a ruby-throated hummingbird outside the window." His voice was whisper-soft though traces of excitement could be heard in his words. "I love those little fellows."

Something in the words brought a rush of memory to Louisa—of another voice and another time in the house on Monroe Street. "I love those little fellows," Chris had always said. The words which were so gentle in Louisa's ears caught at her throat and made an ache there. She might almost have wept at the memory.

"Chris," she said softly. "Oh, my dear Chris." And for a moment—for such a short moment—Johnny was Chris to her. She reached for his hand. He took hers and held it. Together they watched the "little fellow."

The next morning, when Johnny came to open the drapes in room 34, three tubes of brightly-colored sugar water were hanging in the bushes outside the window, and the hummingbird was back—with a friend.

"Thank you, dear," said Louisa. "Thank you so much. It's good to have birds outside my window again."

"Well," Johnny said. "I'm glad you like them. Let's see if we can get some more to come."

After his next day off, there was a feeding tray on the windowsill. Now Louisa could reach out and scatter crumbs and seeds herself.

Johnny brought her the makings of suet balls to hang in the bushes.

"Here, Mrs. B.," he said one morning after breakfast. "Let's get a little messy."

He put three pine cones and a funny-looking bowl of peanut butter on her bed table.

"What's that?" asked Louisa, poking a finger gingerly into the peanut-butter bowl.

"It's not quite what it looks like," said Johnny. "There's more to it than just peanut butter. I mixed in suet and bird seed, too.

"Now what we do," he went on, "is this." He picked up a lump of the sticky stuff in his fingers and stuck it on the pine cone and pushed, so that he worked it well back into the cone, and it was stuck for good.

"There," he said. You finish this one and do the other two. I'll come back to help you clean up and hang them out for you."

Johnny was right. It was messy.

Louisa took small bits of the mixture at first and poked them into the cone, then larger ones and larger still. Before she finished the second one, she had dabs of peanut butter to her wrists, some on the front of her apron—and a smidge or two on the bridge of her nose.

Almost anybody on the staff could have come in, but it was Mrs. Whitehead.

"Oh!" The word was a sharp intake of breath. It contained astonishment and anger.

"Oh, Mrs. B." Mrs. Whitehead's hands flew into the air, almost as if she were defending herself—as if the clutter on the table were some personal attack Louisa had launched against her.

"Would you look at that mess?" she shouted. "Would you just look at that mess!" She jabbed an accusing finger, trembling with anger, at the peanut butter, the seeds, and the pine cones.

"Mrs. B.," she said. "You've done something very, very bad!"

She was off toward the door, shouting, "Aide! We need an aide in this room to clean up a mess. Aide! To room 34, *right now!*"

Almost immediately, there followed the sound of pounding feet in the hallway. When Mrs. Whitehead called for aides, the aides came—in a hurry. Then the nurse came back, followed by the pounding feet.

"You two clean up the table and the floor," commanded Mrs. Whitehead. "I'll clean up the patient." She grabbed a cold wash cloth and began to dab at Louisa.

Confusion washed over Louisa. She hadn't done anything wrong. She had done what Chris told her to do. She had always been a good wife.

She tried to tell Mrs. Whitehead. "Chris brought me these," she said. "It's something I'm making for the birds. I'm supposed to put the peanut butter into the pine cones. And the birds will come and eat it."

The nurse and aides went about their work as if they could not hear what she was saying.

"Chris brought this for me," she repeated. "It's for the birds."

One of the young aides snickered and whispered to the other, "A lot of stuff that goes on around here is for the birds.

Mrs. Whitehead glared at them without missing a stroke in the process of cleaning up Louisa. She sighed and shook her head. "Mrs. Basinger," she said firmly, "your husband has been dead for over a year now. He didn't bring these things to you. I don't know who did, but when I find out . . . !" She made a last rough swipe along the back of Louisa's hand.

"What do we do with this stuff?" The aides gestured toward the pine cones they had stacked in the bowl on top of the peanut butter mixture.

"Throw it away!" said Mrs. Whitehead.

"No!" said Louisa.

The aides swept Johnny's "mess" from the table into the waste basket.

"Birds," said Mrs. Whitehead, "do *not* eat peanut butter." She picked up the wastebasket liner with Louisa's project and disappeared.

I am a person, thought Louisa. *I am a real person. My name is Louisa Nussbaum Hochstetler Basinger.* She stopped to think over the events of the past five minutes.

Maybe, she told herself, *maybe it wasn't Chris who brought me those things. But it was somebody who loved me. Just because that woman doesn't know that birds eat peanut butter doesn't mean that they don't.*

Shortly after the clean-up crew had left, Johnny appeared prepared to look pleased with Louisa's accomplishments. He stopped just inside the door and his pleased expression disappeared. "Louisa, dear," he said. "Where are the suet balls? How did you get the mess cleaned up?"

"I didn't," said Louisa. She wasn't sure whether her voice was going to be angry or tearful. "Somebody else did." She leaned over confidentially. *"Somebody,"* she said, her voice heavy with the significance of it, "who didn't have sense enough to know that birds eat peanut butter."

"Oh, for Pete's sake!" roared Johnny. "Whitehead?"

Louisa pressed her lips together, and nodded a barely perceptible, yes.

Johnny turned angrily and was gone. Louisa could hear the firm march of his steps down the hallway to the nurses' station.

"Whitehead!" he roared. "Where the hell are you?"

Oh, my, thought Louisa. *Such language! I'll have to speak to him about that.* At the same time she was smothering a small chuckle. It wouldn't have been at all nice to laugh about it, she supposed, but she couldn't help wanting to.

Whitehead received a lecture. Johnny would pay the price later, for his "insubordination," or whatever they wanted to call it. In the meantime he told her what he thought of people who got in the way when somebody wanted to do something for "the folks."

"*I* took her the stuff," he said. "And *I* was gonna clean it up—it and her. If you'd have gone in there fifteen minutes later, you'd never have known there was a mess at all.

"Those were *my* things. Louisa and I want them. Where are they?"

There was a muffled sound of protest, but Nurse Whitehead could not overcome the advantage of Johnny's surprise attack. There wasn't much heard from her side.

Then came silence. Louisa could imagine the two of them with their heads in the trash can, fishing for Johnny's "things."

Jessie, in the meantime, out of her room to see about the commotion, poked her head in at Louisa's door. "Sometimes," she said, "that boy almost makes me feel that life is worthwhile again. I sure wish I knew what that was all about."

"That's simple," said Louisa, and told her.

Jessie was in the room and laughing when Johnny returned. He stopped outside the door to shout down the hall, "Birds do eat peanut butter. So *there!*"

The three of them finished the project together, and Johnny went out to hang the cones in the bushes, dangling them at the ends of pieces of brightly-colored yarn. Stepping back to admire his work, he nodded approval of what he had done, then turned to the window to wave at Louisa and Jessie before disappearing back inside, in the direction of whatever projects he had going for other "folks."

"I suppose he'll get in trouble for that," said Jessie.

"For feeding the birds for us?" asked Louisa.

"No . . .I mean for the hassle with Whitehead."

"Oh," said Louisa. A tiny seed of fear was planted at that moment that sprouted and began to grow. Johnny had a job. Trouble in his job might mean that he would lose it. If he lost it, she might not see him again. It was a dreadful thought.

"Don't do it, Johnny," she whispered. "Don't get in trouble for us anymore. Especially don't go and leave us."

"Amen," said Jessie.

I love you Chris . . . Johnny . . . , thought Louisa. *I love you very much.*

But he did get in trouble for grumbling at the other aides when they dawdled in the halls while the food they took to his "folks" got cold.

He got in trouble, too, for spending too much time with his arm around Louisa and Jessie and some of the others—and for thinking it was more important to spend extra time loving them than cleaning floors that he had already mopped once before—on the same day.

Bringing them food caused trouble, too. "What's this?" Nurse Whitehead shouted at him one afternoon. "Cake? Where did Jessie and Mrs. B. get that cake? It's too rich for them. They aren't supposed to have it."

She must have seen this as an opportunity to get even with him for the business about the suet balls. This time it was Johnny who was lectured to in a loud voice at the nurses' station.

Spending extra time at the nursing home when he was off duty created problems for him. "You must understand," they told him, "that the other employees feel that your presence implies that you think they can't perform the job as well as you can."

And he got in trouble for bringing his children to work with him.

Jessie came softly into Louisa's room—she was still in her pajamas—early one morning with the two of them in tow; a runny-nosed little girl of five and a bright-eyed blonde boy who was a year or so younger.

"Hey!" she whispered, shaking Louisa awake. "Get up and help me."

Louisa's eyes flickered open, shut, then open again, as she struggled to move from the land of her dreams to the reality of Parmenter County and room 34.

For just a moment, the house on Monroe Street was there. The picture of Christ knocking on the door was on the wall, and the cherry tree was outside the window. Best of all, Chris's tousled head was in the bed across the room.

"Home," said Louisa. "Oh, praise God, they've let me go home at last . . . at last. Thank you, sweet Jesus."

The wallpaper faded and the white walls of the rest home came into focus, with Jessie's face hovering, and two strange children behind her.

"Ummmmm," moaned Louisa. "What do you want?"

"Miz B.," said Jessie. "Do get up. These are Johnny's kids, and he had to bring them to work this morning. He's not supposed to, and we've got to help him hide them until he can call about a babysitter and get them out of here—probably when he goes on his lunch hour."

Louisa sat up and looked at the two solemn faces. Both were a little dirtier and a little more unkempt than she would have expected in someone whom Johnny loved. "We can't do it," she said. "Two little 'uns like that? Somebody'll find them, sure."

"Well," said Jessie, "after everything Johnny has done for us, we've got to try. Now I've got it all figured out . . . ."

Louisa's current roommate was the absent-minded Bethy, so there was no problem there, as there might have been in Jessie's room, where her roommate loved to tattle.

They would hide the children in Louisa's bathroom until a little later, when visitors started coming. Louisa could say they were some of her great-greats. She had so many, no one would know whether it was true or not.

Louisa had to give that some thought. Lie? Even for Johnny? It was a hard decision to make.

"Well, then," grumbled Jessie, "don't think about it. Just wait 'til the time comes, and do the best you can."

They hid the children in the bathroom. About 8:30—well before visitors were allowed—Nurse Whitehead found them and smiled an unpleasant smile.

"They're Johnny's, aren't they," she demanded, running her tongue back and forth between her teeth while she waited for an answer.

"No," Louisa started to say, but it stuck in her throat and wouldn't come out.

"Never mind," said Whitehead. "It's plain whose they are. They look like him."

"Don't worry," said Jessie, when the nurse had gone, pulling the children, howling, after her. "It's too early for visitors, anyhow. She wouldn't have believed you if you *had* said it."

Jessie and Louisa spent the rest of the day worrying about Johnny and the children.

"Do you suppose he got in trouble?" one of them would ask.

"Why in the world did he have those kids here, anyhow?"

"Where did Chris find children that age?"

"No, Mrs. B., not Chris . . . Johnny. They were *Johnny's* children."

"Where's their mother?"

It was late the next afternoon before Johnny came in to give an explanation. Louisa and Jessie clung together, offering each other hope on Johnny's behalf until then.

"Hi, you two," he said. He looked a little sheepish. "Did I get you in trouble, too?"

"No," answered Jessie, while Louisa shook her head. "There's not much they can do to us."

"Well," he said, "thanks for trying. It was a dumb thing for me to do. I should have just stayed home with them. But the bills have been getting ahead of me lately, and I didn't want to miss a day of work.

"It *was* dumb," he said again, lamely.

"Maybe," said Jessie, "and maybe not." There was a question in her voice that was not in the words themselves.

"Oh, what the heck," said Johnny. "I guess I owe you more of an explanation than that."

His wife had been running around with another man. Now she was gone. Johnny was struggling to make a life for himself and the kids. For the most part it was working. They had a low-rent apartment in a run-down house and a baby sitter who worked for less pay because she had a lot of love but no certification from the state. That morning the sitter had called to say she was sick, and there was no one else to be found before Johnny left for work. He could not leave them alone.

Johnny didn't bring his children to work again. He learned to deal with the problem of caring for them better than that.

There were some things, though, he just couldn't seem to handle any better. He cared too much about his "folks" to treat them just as work. He wanted to spend time, energy, and himself on making them happy by showing them how to have a good life even in the nursing home. He fought the system, and it finally broke him. A morning came when Johnny was supposed to be at work and wasn't.

Louisa lay in bed with her eyes closed, waiting for his warm, boyish voice, so that the too-long nose and the pony tail would be the first thing she saw when she opened them. The beloved voice never came.

It was a cruel blow. Louisa felt as if someone had taken a whip to her soul. After Johnny's departure her mind slipped a little more. Keeping in the present time was harder.

Someone told her once that Johnny had quit to work at a McDonald's restaurant. The pay, they said, was about the same, and there weren't the problems.

Louisa had never been to a McDonald's, and so she never quite understood where her Johnny had gone.

"I do wish," she often said, "that he had come to say good-by."

"I understand why he left," said Jessie. But there was a trace of bitterness in her voice—and more than a little of not understanding. "He cared too much. He couldn't fight them anymore, not even as much as he loved us."

"And so he had to go," she said, adding with the wistful longing of one who has carefully thought through her future, "I wish I could go, too—forever."

Louisa went about the business of what was left to her of life. For a while one main part of that business was remembering Johnny. She wished that he had come to say good-by and she prayed for him daily.

Sometimes she heard bits and pieces of news about him: Johnny was divorced but there was a court fight over the children. Johnny won custody. He had left McDonald's for a better job.

She missed him in the same way she missed home and Chris. Sometimes she closed her eyes and pretended he was there just as she did the double-wedding-ring quilt or her old, lumpy mattress or the cherry tree outside her kitchen window.

Once she made him a Valentine.

It was February 13, and the activities director had insisted that they all report to the day room.

"Today," she said in her cheerleader voice, "we are going to make Valentines . . . Isn't that *nice?* Val . . . en . . . tines!"

Good for you, thought Louisa. *You make them then, because I won't.*

But she changed her mind. It might be a nice thing to have for Johnny in case he came back to say good-by.

She cut a ragged heart from red construction paper. Cutting wasn't easy to do with her hundred-year-old fingers. She glued strips of paper lace unevenly around the edges. Paper lace wasn't easy to see to get straight with hundred-year-old eyes, either. She wrote on it with a trembling hand, "Thank you, Johnny."

"Humph!" said one of the other residents. "That's no Valentine. Valentines are supposed to say, 'I love you.' That ain't no Valentine at all!"

"It is," said Louisa. "It is so, if I want it to be."

She took Johnny's card to her room and hid it in a drawer to wait for him, just in case.

One of the main parts of Louisa's life was the wistful search for another Johnny.

She looked for him in the face of Carrie, a new aide, when the girl first came on the floor.

"Don't I get some kind of training?" asked the bewildered girl.

"Naw," answered one of the other aides. "Come on. I'll show you what to do, and then you do it."

Carrie became an aide cast in the "naw" pattern, under the influence of the "old" aide who had trained her—as if the patients in her care weren't persons of worth.

Louisa looked for Johnny in the face of Tom who, when he first came, seemed gentle and kind and loving. She had hope then. Tom didn't look at all like Johnny. He was more traditional in appearance, with shorter hair neatly combed, and he wore conservative clothing.

But that which was gentle, kind, and loving in Tom disappeared after a while.

"I'm not in the business of taking care of people," Louisa heard him say once. "I take care of bodies where people used to live."

Once that understanding had come to him, Tom treated them all like oversized babies who couldn't hear him or understand what he said, and who couldn't answer him sensibly, either.

He called all of them "honey," or "little lady," or "fellow," or "old boy." Sometimes he called them "naughty girl," or "naughty boy," especially if they soiled their beds. Tom didn't like that at all.

He kept the bodies in his care clean. He kept them fed. He powdered them after what he called "the great disgusting diaper change." He didn't seem to think of them as one sex or another—not men or women, just "bodies."

In exchange for his care, he expected the bodies to smile at him. He would sometimes coax the smile, as one might coax a smile from a baby. He expected his charges and their families to show proper gratitude to him.

I'm not grateful, thought Louisa. *I don't like being treated like an infant. I'm a woman grown, aged and set in my ways. I like a little privacy, and that boy is an offense to all modesty.*

But she learned to still the sense of indignity that came at his approach. She let him help her out of bed and into a wheelchair without shouting "Go away!" She learned to eat the food he brought even though he always said, "Be a good girl and make it all gone, Mrs. B." She learned not to cringe when he said "Bath time! I'm supposed to take you to the shower!"

She learned all that, but she never learned to like it.

Louisa kept looking for someone who would fill the aching hole that Johnny's departure had left inside her. Not all of the aides were like Carrie and Tom. Surely there was another Johnny somewhere.

She looked for him in Nancy Jo, and quickly looked away when she heard Nancy Jo say to a friend, "I don't know about the advantages of progress. Old people used to die before they got so disgusting!"

She looked briefly at the angry aides—the ones who seemed to hate their charges.

"They're afraid of us," Jessie said to her one day. "They know that someday they'll be like us. Maybe they think it's our fault or something. But they're afraid, and that makes them angry."

The angry aides jerked sheets roughly out from under aged bodies when they changed a bed. They came late with food and made cruel remarks when residents couldn't drink the cold coffee or enjoy the cold food.

The very touch of an angry aide was different, and they made a hot shower chilling or a trip to the bathroom a degradation, as if they themselves never knew the need to eliminate, and it was a shame these old people had to be so crude.

Louisa never looked long at the angry ones. For the most part she pretended that they didn't exist.

Louisa thought there might be hope in Andrea. But "Andy" turned out to be one of the worst.

She started out all right. There was depth to her and a charm that made the old folks feel good during the first weeks she was there. Gradually it got to be too depressing for her—and Andy walled herself in to shut them out.

For Andy, they went from people to things.

"Bath time," Andy would say, in much the same way that one might announce that it was time to wash the dishes.

Lift an arm.

Remove the clothes.

Cover the old thing with a blanket.

Put the old thing in a molded plastic shower chair.

Push it down the hall.

In the shower room another aide would join her. There, one on each side of the chair, they gave an efficient shower.

Whip off the blanket.

Push the chair and its contents under the spray to get them wet.

Pull them back out.

Soap the thing in the chair.

Shove it back under for a quick rinse.

Pat if off with an already-damp towel, and then take it back to its room and put some clean clothes on it.

It was quick, neat . . . efficient . . . and hateful.

Other aides came and went. Whatever they seemed to be like, Louisa always gave them a hopeful examination. They all failed her.

They weren't all angry . . . or uncaring . . . or insensitive, of course. Many of them cared. They knew how to speak to the old people. They knew how to offer comfort and warmth. But they weren't Johnny.

Louisa never found another Johnny. She only found people doing a job.

It was never enough to satisfy her soul's needs.

13

THE FIGHT

Louisa woke and Johnny wasn't there. She sighed heavily. It had happened so many times that the passing of weeks and months had blunted the pain—as if whatever knife was being twisted inside her had grown dull from overuse. Nevertheless, it was still there.

I suppose, she thought, easing back the covers and sliding her feet over the edge, *I suppose I'll die with that pain inside me. He was such a special person.*

There was always that other, extra little pain. *If only he had cared enough to come and say good-by.*

Well, she told herself firmly, *he didn't. And that is that.*

Looking around her room, Louisa saw the few spots of clutter. There was never anything *real* for the residents to do to care for themselves. Their rooms were cleaned, their beds made. They were helped into wheelchairs and into bed. If they spilled anything, someone else wiped it up.

Once in a while somebody missed picking something up, and Louisa would get to do it herself. The sight of those spots of clutter delighted her.

The ears and the necktie on the purple elephant were all twisted again. There was a rumpled facial tissue that had missed the wastebasket. Two of the pictures on the dresser had gotten out of place.

Somebody had picked them up to look at them, and put each back where the other should have been.

Well, thought Louisa, *I see what I can do this morning. This room needs to be tidied.*

Louisa, pleased with herself and the world, tidied.

She settled herself firmly into her wheelchair, rolled across to the purple elephant, and carefully straightened its tie and ears. Then she dusted the windowsill. She couldn't see clearly enough to know but there might be enough small specks to justify pulling out her handkerchief and using it for a dust cloth.

When the windowsill was straightened and dusted, she congratulated herself on having done for herself, then rolled toward the tissue.

Carefully, taking every precaution against falling, she bent over. She held to the wheelchair and the night stand, then freed one hand, reached for the rumpled paper hanky, and deposited it in the wastebasket.

"There," she said, "that looks much better."

Finally, there was the top of the dresser to see to. She put the pictures back in their respective places. Louisa was a woman who liked things the way she liked them—and where she liked pictures was in the spots she had assigned to them.

"Ah," she said, with a wistful wish that she could be in her own home again, taking care of herself.

"Ah-h, it's so nice to have a dab of cleaning and tidying to do."

And then came Jessie.

Every time Jessie wheeled herself through the door, Louisa sensed, more than she could see with her failing sight, that Jessie was deteriorating physically more and more.

She sits tired these days, thought Louisa. *There used to be a proud set to her shoulders and a dignity about the way she carried her head. Her movements used to be willing and quick.*

"Good morning, Louisa, dear. Shall we have a bite of breakfast together today?"

Louisa looked across at her sleeping roommate. "That would be very nice," she said. "My room or yours?"

"Mine, I think," said Jessie. "It's more private."

Louisa took her cherished dishes from the night stand, gave them a pat, and tucked them carefully into the wheelchair beside her.

Jessie was about to turn and lead the way from the room when her eye fell on the ghastly purple elephant.

"Oh my," she said. "His tie is crooked again . . . and those funny ears just never do stay straight. Here . . . ," she wheeled herself toward the windowsill, "let me fix him." And she had Louisa's purple treasure in her lap, stroking, cuddling, fixing, making a fuss.

"Poor fellow . . . you have more trouble with your ears and your tie."

Wait! cried something in Louisa's heart. *Don't do that. He's mine and I fixed him just the way I wanted him. He's mine!*

Not only was he arranged the way she wanted him, she was the one who had defended him against the folk who wanted to laugh at a ghastly purple elephant on an old lady's windowsill. She was the one who liked him best.

How does one explain to a well-meaning friend who rearranges pictures and purple elephants that her well-meant action has shaken something deep inside?

He's mine, she thought. *Jessie should leave him alone!*

"He's mine!" she wailed. "He's *mine!* Leave him alone!"

Forgetting that her chair would roll, Louisa struggled to her feet and reached for the elephant. Snatching him from Jessie's lap, she clutched him to her with trembling arms, repeated, *"Mine!"* and backed away from Jessie, who suddenly seemed a threat.

"Well, I didn't *mean* anything by it, Mrs. Fussbudget," said Jessie. "I certainly didn't intend to upset you."

"Mine," whispered Louisa into a purple ear.

"Yes, he's yours. And I certainly won't touch him again."

"Mine," said Louisa, touching the pink end of the purple trunk.

"I heard you," yelled Jessie. "Don't worry. I'm going to my room. I'll eat breakfast alone. Don't you bother coming."

She turned her chair angrily and was gone.

Be that way, then, thought Louisa. *I can eat here well enough. It's not as if I didn't have dishes of my own.* She settled the dilapidated purple animal back into his place on the windowsill.

"Mine," she whispered softly into the lonely air.

It surprised her, somehow, to discover just how lonely it was. Her roommate was now wide awake after the commotion and peering out of her blankets with two beady eyes. Bethy was almost worse than no one at all. Louisa was still too alert to really enjoy the company of a woman who couldn't remember things as far back as a minute-and-a-half ago.

Too able to think clearly for the dull ones . . . a little too slow for others . . . too able to remember for some . . . too old for that one . . . but too young for some of the others.

Wrong, she thought. *I'm all wrong for everybody.*

Except Jessie. Now that, too, was spoiled.

"*Good* morning." An aide came through the door with breakfast. "How are you girls this morning?"

Louisa was too busy with her own thoughts to object, "I'm not a *girl.*"

But not today. It was Bethy who answered. "I'm okay. But she's not so good. She just had a fight with Jessie over that dumb elephant, and now Jessie don't like her no more."

There was something in Bethy's voice that sounded almost pleased. "She don't like you no more, and she ain't never gonna like you again."

The words created a strange feeling for Louisa, as though her soul were in the midst of a severe winter—and icicles hung from her heart.

Oh, the loneliness of it.

"Bring my breakfast to room 48, please," said Louisa to the bustling aide. She eased herself into her chair and was gone.

Knock, knock. "Jessie," she called, and knocked again. "Jessie?"

The only answer was a deliberate sniff.

" . . . and she ain't never gonna like you again" echoed down the hall to hang in the doorway, daring Louisa to enter.

"Jessie," she called again, softly, and went in.

Jessie's back was to the door. Her breakfast was behind her, as if the position were a deliberate attempt to ignore her visitor.

It wasn't going to be at all easy.

"I'm sorry," said Louisa. "I don't know what got into me."

No reply.

"It's just that they leave us so little here that is really us."

No reply.

"Doesn't 'I'm sorry' help? Even a little?"

No reply.

"Jessie, I need you for a friend." It was very hard for Louisa to humble herself to say this. "The others are all wrong for me."

Jessie's shoulders moved. Was she bored? Was she angry? Or was she softening?

"Mrs. B!" In came the breakfast aide, loud, demanding.

"Mrs. B., you are going to have to go back to your own room for breakfast. I had it all laid out already when you left, and I'm not about to move it." The aide's words came thick and fast, overwhelming Louisa.

"Jessie?" she said, hopeful of forgiveness.

"Come on. Right now," said the aide, and grabbed Louisa's wheelchair to push her out of the room.

"Wait!" commanded Louisa, but her chair kept moving, as though the aide had not heard.

"Wait! This is important. I have to talk to Jessie. I have to have my friend back!"

The chair didn't slow. Louisa tried to grab the wheels and couldn't. "Wait!"

"Damn it!" said Jessie from behind them. "Can't you hear the woman? Wait!"

What was it about Jessie that captured respect, even from her caretakers? Louisa didn't know, but there was certainly something. The chair slowed, and the aide turned.

"Ladies," she said, "I am a very busy woman. I have fifty breakfasts to deliver this morning. Some of those breakfasts have to be fed to people." There was more weariness than anger in her voice. "I just don't have time to set a breakfast up in one place, then move it to another. No matter how badly you want it done."

She started out the door with Louisa.

But by that time Jessie was there, and she caught the chair against her own chair to stop it.

"Louisa," she said, "will eat here with me if she chooses to do so. If you are too damn lazy to walk down the hall to bring her food, then I'll share mine with her."

There was a brief pause while all three of them stared at each other. "Good-by," said Jessie and the aide left.

"Come on," Jessie said. "Let's eat."

They were at opposite sides of Jessie's little table, breaking soggy, cold toast into bite-sized bits and sipping half-cups of cold coffee when the aide returned with Louisa's tray. She said nothing, just plunked it down.

"People change their minds, sometimes," said Jessie. "Don't they?"

It was the closest she ever came to an apology.

"Why," asked Louisa, "did you change yours?"

Jessie smiled. "Well, I figure we've been friends for quite a spell, and if I want to grumble at you now and again—or if I want to get just a bit mad at you—then that's my business and my privilege. But I just don't take it kindly when anybody else does it."

The two of them went back to their soggy toast and their cold coffee.

"I won't fuss at you about little things like that any more," said Louisa before she left.

"Maybe you will, maybe you won't. It'll work out either way. And I'll try to remember not to touch your things without asking," Jessie promised, straightening Louisa's crocheted lap robe over the older woman's knees. "I really do understand how you feel about a thing like that."

"And besides," she added, her usual quiet dignity overshadowed by shyness for a moment, "I don't quite know what I'd do without you. I *need* at least one close friend. I've always been that way."

"I can't be friends with the others." Her hand made a sweeping gesture that included all of the other residents. "They keep dying—or getting so senile that there's no talking to them—or getting so feeble that there's hardly anything left of them physically . . . .

"Louisa, my friend, at least you keep hanging in there. I don't honestly think I could go on living without you."

"Oh, pshaw!" said Louisa.

The two of them were friends again, and in that friendship they clung together and watched the others pass by.

Uncle Rudy carried on long conversations with people only he could hear.

William always wore a hat that was just a bit too large for him. Indoors and out, he had that hat on, perched on the tips of his ears and flattening them forward, so he had the look of a mournful hound holding its ears up in curiosity.

William wasn't curious or mournful. There wasn't enough of him left, mentally, for that. While his ears looked curious, his face wore an expression of weary resignation.

William was a wanderer. Every day or so someone would have to go out to look for him, after he had slipped out the door in the company of friendly visitors. Every day or so they had to bring him back frightened, tears running down his cheeks, whimpering, "Why do I have to come here? What is this place? Who are you?"

Nettie sat in a rocker that her family had put in the day room for her. If someone else sat in the chair or if they happened to bump into it while Nettie was sitting there, she would leap toward them with her cane as fast as a ninety-three-year-old woman could leap. Then she would whack the offender's shoulders or backside or head with her cane if they couldn't move fast enough to get out of her way.

They watched the gentle, pleasant Johnson woman slip into senility as, immediately after she moved in, she cut herself off from any of the emotional ties that had held her to life.

"Miz Johnson's family doesn't visit her much, but she never complains," observed Louisa to Jessie one afternoon.

"No," said Jessie. "Looks to me like she's cutting herself off from all the people she's cared about."

When Mrs. Johnson's oldest son died, she didn't seem too upset by it. "He was a nice boy," was all she said, as if he had been a neighbor or an acquaintance instead of her son.

"The fact that someone dies is part of life," said Jessie. "Like the final curtain is an important part of a play.

"But Miz Johnson isn't taking part in life anymore. All she knows to be is old, and that's not really living. So even when someone dies, it isn't important to her.

"You know, Louisa, dear," she said, "dying isn't the opposite of life. Old age is. Life and death have a certain dignity about them. But old age—old age is like somebody's making fun of life and death both."

Louisa frowned. It sounded profound and important to Jessie. But she really didn't understand it.

They watched the afternoon poker game. All the players sat in the same spot every day, saying the same things, and eating the same snacks.

"My lands," said Ted at every deal, "I got a great hand this time—five aces!"

"Peanuts, anyone?" George said.

"No, thanks, but I'd like one of them mints if you've a mind."

"Let's quit the gab and get on with the game!" said Samuel.

If one of them were missing, the others could play the game all right, but they had a terrible time with conversation, just as if in a play one of the lead actors missed a performance.

Louisa and Jessie listened while the poker players talked—and they listened to others as well.

Over and over Gib Shamell told the story of moving his wife and small family to a new house when he was a young man of twenty-four.

"We'd been livin' in a log house over by Galion, and I found us a better place to rent t'other side of town. Only way to move our stuff was to walk and carry it. Which was all right, 'cause we didn't have that much anyhow.

"Well, we made this one trip where my share of the load was a change of clothes and the baby. Which was fine with me. He was a right pert little feller and spent most of the trip grinnin' at me.

"But we come to this one crick we had to cross, and the only way over was to walk on these here rocks that folks had put acrost the shallow part.

"Well, I was doing fine, but one of them rocks had sure enough got itself slipperied up with some moss, and I no sooner got a foot on that rock than I slipped off again, and wellnigh fell into that crick.

"Now, I needed a hand to balance myself, and I had to make a quick decision. Which hand to use—the one that held my clothes, or the one that held the baby.

"Well, sir, I ended up dropping the baby, and using that hand to steady myself.

"I picked him up again, of course, just fished him out the water, a-screamin' and a'squallin'—and carried him on acrost the stream.

"My wife was waitin' for me on t'other side, just a-carryin' on about me droppin' the baby.

"I tell you, I never could get that woman to understand why I done it that way. You see, I reckoned we could always get another baby—but by damn, that was the only good suit of clothes I had!"

Gib would tell the story—and smile—and five minutes or so later, he would lean toward them to say, "Did I ever tell you ladies about the time I dropped the baby in the crick?"

It was as though he had retreated in time and was stuck at that peculiar moment, fated to live it over and over.

Whenever he asked the question, Jessie and Louisa would sigh, and either leave—or listen again.

They listened as well to Julie, who loved to talk about the wild parties a younger Julie had been involved in.

"I used to play the guitar and my husband played the fiddle," Julie would tell them. When we played together in the evenings, the neighbors would hear and come in to dance.

"A lot of times I would fix a little something to drink, not whiskey or anything. We never cared for whiskey. But something. We would get to having a real party." Her eyes shone with the memory.

"The only problem was . . . ," Julie grinned sheepishly, "that those parties got a little louder and a little louder every night, until finally they got so loud that we had to move to get away from them!" She would throw back her head and laugh.

The problem with Julie's stories was that you could never tell whether they were true or not. Past, present, future, Julie had a tendency to invent things.

"My daughter was here yesterday and took me out to dinner," she would volunteer, without remembering that Louisa and Jessie had been sitting with her during the very meal she mentioned.

Noticing her new lap robe and not able to explain where she got it, Julie would say, "This here quilt has been in my family for years. It was give to me by my great-grandma, who got it from her great-grandma, who was the one who made it," when in reality the blanket was on loan to her from an aide who had tired of hearing her complain about cold knees.

"Tomorrow I'm gonna go to the store and get me some vittles," when everyone but Julie knew that she was not permitted to leave the building.

As Jessie and Louisa watched the others and listened to them, they stayed together, thankful for each other and for minds that were still alert.

And then the terrible thing happened—the tiny, little, terrible thing that Louisa never noticed, but Jessie did.

It was all about the purple elephant again—Louisa's precious purple elephant that she had defended and fought for: the crazy, ugly purple elephant that the two of them had argued over which had almost spoiled their friendship.

Jessie knew how Louisa felt about that elephant. She didn't intend to touch it again. She forgot.

They had been sitting by the window in Louisa's room. It was spring, and there were birds about. They were reminded of

Johnny and how he used to feed the birds there. They were remembering a past that they had shared and it was good.

It was so good that Jessie forgot her good intentions about the purple elephant. She reached out to pick it up and pull it into her lap to straighten the ears and tie.

At first Louisa didn't notice. Jessie realized what she had done. "Oh, my God," she thought. "We're going to have trouble again!"

She was trying to slip the stuffed animal back, hoping that Louisa hadn't noticed, but Louisa turned and saw it there in Jessie's hands.

Louisa looked at the animal for a long moment. "What is that?" she asked, peering, as though her eyes weren't quite able to see the thing well enough to identify it.

"It's . . . it's your elephant," said Jessie, more frightened than the occasion demanded. Her heart had leaped, pounding, into her throat and ears, and her hands trembled as she held the stuffed purple beast out toward Louisa.

Louisa took it to examine more closely. "Oh," she said. "It's quite nice. Is it yours?"

And that was the terrible thing that happened. Louisa wasn't trying to be funny or sarcastic. She meant it.

In that strange, turned-around moment, Jessie somehow knew that the day was coming—and coming soon—when Louisa was going to be just like the others.

Jessie took the purple elephant from her friend and set it back on the windowsill. She straightened both ears and tie.

"No, Louisa dear," she said. "It's yours." She sank into her chair as if all the defeat and hurt that a lifetime had given her had come back to haunt her.

After a moment, Jessie straightened her shoulders as if she had made herself a promise. When she spoke again, there was a finality about it.

"Good-by," she said. "Good-by, Louisa." The tears that she would not permit to come to her eyes could be heard in her voice.

"Good-by."

14

JESSIE LEAVES, JOHNNY RETURNS

The next morning Jessie was dead.

The rumors were that she might have been saving her sleeping capsules for several weeks, and that she might have taken them all at once.

People remembered how often she had said that death was preferable to life.

It was said that she had had a terrible argument with Louisa, and that was what had brought it on.

Someone said that she had crawled into bed that night muttering something about purple elephants, and someone else remembered the time Jessie got hit by a car.

But rumor, in a place like the Parmenter County Home, isn't something that is *believed*. It's more something that is talked about.

Officially, the residents were told that Jessie Henderson's heart had worn out, and she had died quietly in her sleep. Official stories are not always believed, either.

Louisa knew nothing of the controversy at first. She awoke that morning as she always did. First came the realization that she was old, then the understanding of where she was, then the remembering that Chris was dead and Johnny had left.

Once she had worked through the past to the present, her first thought was: "Well, let's see, shall I have Jessie here for breakfast? Or shall I go to her room?"

When Jessie did not come to Louisa, her question was answered. As soon as an aide had helped her to dress, she set off.

"Send my breakfast to room 48," said Louisa, and wondered at the sad look that was the aide's only answer.

When she got to room 48, Jessie's bed was freshly made. There was no sign of her friend.

"Jessie?" called Louisa. "Whooo-ooooo. Jessiiiiiie?"

Louisa didn't notice that Jessie's possessions had been packed and removed.

"Jessie?"

Well, she thought, *reckon I'll just sit a spell and wait for her.*

She sat until an aide came hurrying in with a bucket and a mop.

"Hullo there, Miz B.," said the aide. "What you doin' in *this* room this mornin'?"

Something in the words might have warned Louisa if she had paid more attention to them and to the way they were said. She noticed, though, that it was a foolish question.

"I'm waiting," she said, "to have breakfast with Jessie. Like I *always* do." There was an edge of impatience in the way she spoke. It echoed against the empty walls of the room, sharpened itself there and came back at her in the aide's voice.

"Well, you gonna have one long wait, Miz B.," he said. "One hell of a long wait." He laughed cruelly. "Come on, now. You clear out of here. I've got to finish this room. Parmenter County has a waiting list, you know, and there'll be somebody wanting to get one of their old folks moved in."

If her thought processes had not been so painfully slowed, Louisa might have figured it all out by then. As it was, she didn't understand. She knew that something was wrong. But she had no idea what it could be.

"I guess I'll just have to go look for her."

Louisa went whoo-ooooing softly down the hall. "Jessie?" she called, as she passed each door. "Have you seen Jessie?"

As no answer came, she sensed that something was terribly wrong.

It was Julie who came to the rescue. When Louisa looked into her room, Julie had an answer. "Yes, indeed. I just saw her down in the day room."

Julie was just coming from her bathroom and still in her pajamas. Her wheelchair was still parked in the corner where she had left it the night before. She had offered hope even though she could not have seen Jessie in the day room that morning.

Louisa picked up that hope like a warm shawl someone had thrown to her on a chilly evening, wrapped it around herself, and wheeled off down the hall as fast as she could go.

At the double doors she slowed, more than half afraid to enter, in case Julie was wrong.

Julie was wrong.

Jessie was not in the day room.

"I don't believe I'm going to find her," said Louisa to herself. "How can that be?"

"William," she said. "Have you seen Jessie?"

William lifted his bowed head to peer out from under the brim of his too-large hat. "Who are you?" was his only answer.

"Gib," said Louisa. "Have you seen Jessie?"

Gib considered. "No," he said deliberately. "I don't reckon I have." His eyes lit up. "But have I told you the story about how I dropped the baby in the . . . ."

Louisa had turned away and missed the conclusion of the question she had heard before.

"You," she said to a resident she didn't know. "Have you seen Jessie Henderson?"

"A," said the resident, "B . . . C . . . D . . .E, F, G . . . ."

"Oh, dear God," said Louisa. The words were softly spoken, but they came from the cry of anguish inside her.

"Miz Johnson . . . *please,* Miz Johnson, have you seen Jessie?

"Yes," said the gentle woman.

"Where?" demanded Louisa.

"I saw her this morning. They wheeled her out. I think she's dead."

Deaddeaddeaddeaddead . . . The word caught inside Louisa's mind and echoed back and forth from one side of her head to the other. *Deaddeaddeaddeaddead.*

That couldn't be. Jessie was strong and healthy. Yesterday, she had been full of life. Jessie was her friend. She needed her. Louisa couldn't bear the loss of another friend.

She turned to search the room for someone who might have an answer she could accept.

"There's Gib. Maybe he'll know. I'll ask him."

"Have you seen Jessie?"

"No . . . I don't reckon I have." His eyes lit up. "But have I told you . . . "

"William? Jessie? . . .Have you seen her?"

"Who are you?"

"You!" to another resident. "Have you seen Jessie Henderson?"

"Bring me something warm to cover my arms. My arms are cold. Bring me something warm. Hurry up! Please!"

"Aaaaaaah!" broke from Louisa, a cry of anguish that came from her soul. Tears she did not want to shed forced themselves to her eyes and down her cheeks.

Louisa felt the pain of Jessie's absence as if her whole being had suddenly grown much heavier. Her arms were too heavy to move. Her feet were too heavy to shuffle along the floor to move the wheelchair. Her shoulders were too heavy to do anything but sag.

Weighted down, she sat in her wheelchair and waited, without thought or understanding—except for the strange word *deaddeaddeaddeaddead* that came sometimes to her unbidden.

It was there toward noon Nurse Whitehead found her. "Mrs. B.," she said, "what are you doing here? I found your breakfast untouched in your room, and you haven't taken your morning medication."

Louisa's head was so heavy she couldn't raise it to look at the nurse.

"Don't be obstinate, Mrs. B. Answer me. What are you doing here?"

Her chin was too heavy to move and form words. She tried. All she accomplished was a barely-perceptible up and down movement of the lower jaw that communicated nothing.

"Very well," said Nurse Whitehead. "If that's the way you want it. Come on."

She stepped firmly around the chair and wheeled Louisa home to room 34.

It was just as well that Louisa was too overwhelmed by her pain to understand the comments that were whispered as they passed.

"I've always *thought* there must be old folks who kill themselves."

"Now, we don't really know that it was . . . "

" . . . dead, she was, and smiling more than I've ever seen her . . . ."

"She must have taken quite a few of them . . . ."

"How do you suppose she saved them up without anybody finding out?"

"That Jessie was a smart old girl."

"But we don't *know* that it was . . . ."

"She was too healthy yesterday to be dead today, unless she . . . ."

The doctor said it was heart failure . . . ."

"I read an article somewhere that said old age is by far the most usual time for suicide."

"The official report . . . ."

Louisa went to bed to rest, and when she was able to talk again, she asked if Jessie were really dead.

"Yes," they said.

She asked several of them, just to be sure. The answer was always the same. "Yes . . . she died in her sleep."

Louisa asked to be visited by a local minister. She needed to talk to someone who shared her faith.

"Sure, I'll get one for you," said Whitehead. "What kind do you want?"

"A Christian minister," said Louisa, wondering that the nurse wouldn't know that. "Someone who loves the Lord."

Three or four days later, he came.

His voice was soft, and his manner comforting.

"Good morning," he said, in his soft, honey-sweet way. "I am Reverend Swanson."

"How do you do," said Louisa from her bed. She had been spending much of her time resting.

"They told me you wanted a minister. What can I do for you?"

"Talk to me," said Louisa. "About God. And about God's love."

"Oh," said the minister. "Well . . . ," he seemed uncomfortable, as if that subject was not what he had expected. He shuffled his feet.

"Sit down," said Louisa, pointing to the uncomfortable chair at her bedside.

He was tall and thin, she noticed, and dressed in black. He folded himself into the chair and leaned toward her.

Seventy years and more had suddenly faded and Louisa remembered another visit.

"What do you want this time, Elder Specht?" asked Louisa.

Reverend Swanson was accustomed to visiting with old people. He didn't show any surprise at her use of another name.

"What do you want this time?" she repeated, and her thoughts went back to the time when Elder Specht had visited her after her divorce from Amos.

She became aware that Reverend Swanson was speaking to her. But she had no idea what he had been talking about.

"And that's the way I see it," said Reverend Swanson, standing to take his leave. He crossed to her bed and patted her hand. "Does it help any?"

Oh, dear, thought Louisa. *I think I missed my visit with a minister.*

Part of her could have cried—but another part felt rather silly about the visit and wanted to laugh. It balanced out.

"Well," she said, "yes . . . I think so. And thank you very much for coming." She lifted her hand for him to shake.

She got out of bed after he left and wheeled over to look out the window. "Sometimes," she said to the purple elephant, "I wonder about me!"

Whimsy was lost in a wave of sadness. "I wonder," she added, touching a finger to the purple trunk, "if I'm accomplishing anything at all these last years."

It was a question that was about to have an answer.

When Louisa opened her eyes following a nap that afternoon, she thought that she could see birds on her windowsill. They were hopping and pecking on the feeding tray that Johnny had fixed for her that time long ago.

Oh, my, she thought, *isn't that nice?*

For a brief moment—foolish thought, old woman—it seemed that Johnny must still be working there, and it was he who had put food for them in the tray.

As usual, she worked her way back through yesterday to today, as she always had to do now—even if she had just been napping—and she knew that Johnny was gone; Chris and Jessie were dead, and she was alone.

Foolish old woman, she thought.

"Hello, there," said Johnny

Oh, my, thought Louisa. *I'm having more trouble than usual about keeping things straight. I must remember how it really is. Chris is dead. Jessie died, too. And Johnny is gone.*

"There . . . I've got it."

"Mrs. B.," said Johnny. "There's someone I'd like you to meet."

"Oh, pshaw," said Louisa. "I'm getting just like that nice Uncle Rudy. I'm starting to hear voices!"

Johnny leaned over the bed, then, and ran his fingers gently through her strings of yellow-white hair. "Mrs. B., you aren't hearing voices. It's me."

Louisa rolled over from side to back and lay staring up at him. What miracle had brought him to her? Was she dying?

"Chris?" she said. Then, "Chris! Oh, my dear, dear Chris!" Small tears filled her eyes and lay there, sparkling at Johnny, as she raised her arms to offer him a hug.

He bent to receive it, whispering, "Not Chris, Mrs. B. Not this time. It's Johnny."

He held her as tight as he dared, then kept her hand and stood looking down at her. The whisper had brought no reaction, and he spoke louder. "I'm *Johnny*. Do you remember?"

Of course she remembered. It took her time, that's all.

She remembered his dark eyes and the warm glow in them—almost as well as if she could still see them in her darkened room.

She remembered his smile, touching it with her fingertips, to be sure it was still there, and still the same.

"I don't see quite as well as I used to," she apologized.

"I came back," he said, "to thank you."

Louisa felt flustered by that. "Thank *me?*" she said. "Oh, pshaw!"

"I mean it, Mrs. B. You meant a lot to me when I worked here. You were always trying to help me with something or other—like the time with the kids and all. I never could do half for you what I wanted to.

"But I want you to know that my life is working out a lot better now. I got a good job. I'm working as activities director in a little rest home over in Richland County."

For a moment Louisa could see Johnny acting the cheer leader. But it wouldn't be like that, of course, not if her Johnny was doing the job. Johnny would have birds and love and laughter and music.

"I really like that kind of work," he finished.

"I got married again, too," he said. "My wife is a real good mother for the kids."

"And a real good wife for me." He waved, and a young woman with a warm, gentle touch crossed the room to stand beside him and take Louisa's hand.

"This is Rachel," said Johnny.

How beautiful, thought Louisa. *After the divorce and all the pain and turmoil he had, he found someone else to love him and the children.*

It was beautiful. Louisa knew just how beautiful, because she remembered how Chris had come to her after her divorce. So it was that Louisa understood Johnny's heart.

"I believe," she said, "that God sent Rachel to you to love you and your children. And I will pray for his finest blessings for both of you." It was Louisa's turn to pat *their* hands.

"Thanks," said Johnny.

"Thank you," Rachel said.

They hugged her and were leaving when a thought struck Louisa. She wasn't sure where it came from. It was something she had to remember, and everyone knew that her memory wasn't much anymore.

"Wait!" said Louisa. "Wait! I have something for you."

She reached into a drawer by her bed and pulled it out—a ragged heart cut from red construction paper and decorated with strips of wrinkled paper lace.

"Here," she said. "I made it for you on Valentine's Day—well, some Valentine's Day or other." Her voice was apologetic. "I don't remember just which one."

Johnny read the message in the trembling letters, and his eyes glistened.

"I'm sorry," he said. "I'm sorry I didn't come back sooner. I won't stay away so long again."

With those words they were gone.

Louisa was not quite so lonely anymore. Johnny had come back to say good-by. It proved to her that good things in life were possible after the hundred-year mark.

15

NOT REALLY LOUISA

If Johnny came back to see her again, Louisa never knew it.

As she neared the age of one hundred and six, her bad times grew in length and frequency. That which Jessie had feared most before she died had happened. Louisa was becoming like the other residents of the nursing home.

Louisa realized, at times, that something was happening.

She knew her vision was getting weaker, until finally she could no longer read her Bible—not even with the help of the magnifying glass she had been using for years.

The Bible was left open on a table, and Louisa reached out to touch it often, as if touching would help her to remember the words that were engraved in her heart.

"I will never leave thee nor forsake thee."

"I have called thee by thy name. Thou art mine."

"He that liveth and believeth in me shall never die."

"Oh, sweet Jesus," prayed Louisa, "my dear, my beloved, my own precious Friend. Please, Lord, now that I am forgetting so many things, don't let me forget the Word that I have read. Let it remain still with me in my heart."

And it was so. After over ninety years of reading that Word, it did not leave her but was a comfort to her in the closing months of her life.

She knew that she was losing her hearing too. Near the end of her life, conversation with Louisa was nearly impossible. A sentence had to be spoken very loudly, one word at a time. It was necessary to wait and be sure she had heard a word before the next was said. And after she had heard the words, it took time for her to understand them before she could answer.

One of the great-greats came, a handsome boy—though Louisa couldn't see to know that he was handsome. He wanted so much to ask her about the houses she had lived in.

"What was a log cabin really like, Gramma?" he asked.

Louisa looked at him hard, frowning. None of his words had got through to her.

"Ask her again, Scotty. More slowly this time. Talk real slow and loud and plain so she can understand you," said the boy's grandfather, who was standing by.

"What . . . was . . . a . . . log cabin . . . like, Gramma?" he said, struggling with the words to make her understand them.

Still she frowned, shaking her head.

"WHAT . . . WAS . . . A . . . LOG . . .CABIN . . .LIKE?" There was frustration in his voice. They had told him she would know the answer to his question. But he couldn't even get her to hear the question.

Louisa smiled. He had got through to her, at last. She had sensed enough words to answer young Scotty.

"Yes, I like log cabins. I like them very much." She smiled again, and patted his hand.

"You're a good boy." She would have called him by name if she could have remembered for sure what it was. "I like log cabins just fine," she said, to make up for not knowing his name.

Scotty shrugged his shoulders, rolled his eyes, and left.

Fortunately for Louisa, she hadn't seen his reaction and she never knew his impatience with an aged and bothersome great-grandmother.

The other visitors stayed with her a bit longer. They had learned how to handle conversation when Louisa was present.

Some of them didn't say anything at all to her—talking to each other instead. Or they held her hand, patted her shoulder, and said nothing at all. Others would say one or two words, loud and slow, so she could be sure to catch them.

"WANT a COOKIE?"

"Yes, thanks," Louisa would say. She still enjoyed her food.

"THIS IS JENNIE . . . JEN . . . NIE."

"Hello, Jane," Louisa would answer. "Pleased to meet you."

That was the extent of Louisa's conversation from visitors in the last months of her life. She tried very hard not to be hurt.

When Louisa's aged eyes and ears began to have problems, so did her one-hundred-six-year-old mind. Louisa never fully realized that.

Mentally, she had begun slipping when Chris died, of course. After his death there had always been bad moments when she had to fight to keep her thinking clear—and no matter how she fought, sometimes she couldn't make it.

Then when Johnny left, and she lost him, too—and with him, lost Chris once again—she lost more of herself.

Jessie's dying had cost her as well.

In the end, it was as though the years had scored too many points against her and won.

Much of the time Louisa was no longer Louisa.

She would have hated this part of her aging if she had realized.

She spent most of her time in sleep.

"Only lazy folks nap during the day," she would have said. "What a shameful waste of time."

When visitors came, she hardly ever recognized them.

"Hello, Papa," she would say to Wallace.

"Pleased to meet you," to Mary.

"Jessie . . . Jessie, do stop in and visit a minute," to a passing resident.

She complained bitterly at Wallace and Mary and begged once again to go home to plant her garden.

The aides came sometimes, put her in her wheelchair and pushed her down to the day room to sit in the vacant-eyed line-up.

Most of all, she would have hated the plastic bag attached to her chair on those days—and the times when aides had to change her and her bed linens.

Mercifully, Louisa never knew about those things. That period in her life was short.

On July 5, 1975—a Saturday—Louisa woke, alert, and knew that her final day had come at last. She was 106 years old. The morning had dawned in a burst of glory. Sunlight came over the rim of the horizon to shine through Louisa's window— past the African violet and the faded purple elephant on the windowsill, past the rumpled bed of her roommate, across the brown-flecked tiles of the floor, and onto her bed.

Her mind was clear for the first time in many days. The last few days—or was it weeks—or months—had been worse than ever before.

I can remember how it went, she thought, *but not how long it took.*

The first step—why could she remember it so easily now?—the first step had been when they confined her to a wheelchair.

"No more walks, Louisa," a young doctor had insisted. From that time on, they had fastened her into the chair with a heavy, green strap around both her reluctant body and the chair. It was buckled in the back where she could not reach.

Jessie had been with her in those days. Even with Jessie there, Louisa had been bothered by an oddly frightening thought. She began to feel like a harnessed monkey, dangling at the end of some unnamed organ grinder's chain—only she was not able to dance for their amusement.

About the time Johnny had come to visit her, they had changed her schedule to half a day in bed and half a day in the wheelchair.

After Louisa had a series of strokes, the nursing home staff had made her stay in bed almost all the time.

When she first realized what this day would bring, joy grew inside her like the uncurling of a rosebud into full flower. The beauty and the fragrance of that joy whispered through her, ca-ressing the tips of her gnarled fingers, spreading to the soles of her worn feet, bringing tears to her eyes and her cheeks.

"Thank you, Lord," she said.

She knew it was the day because they were standing by her bed when she first opened her eyes. Her surprise at seeing them made her heart beat faster and move to her throat to thump there.

Slowly, as if sudden movement might frighten them away, Louisa turned her head toward them.

"Papa?" she said. "Mama?" How did you get here? What are you . . . ?

"And Mabel . . . oh, of course I recognize you. All of you. I'm so glad to see you!"

For only a moment Louisa's face, beneath its crown of gold-tinted white hair, looked puzzled. "And you are . . . you are . . . Oh, I remember. You're Dinah Anne, Geraldine's girl who was in the car wreck in Oregon." Louisa extended a hand, as if in greeting.

"Hello, dear child." She paused and seemed to be listening, then smiled. "Well," she said, "it was a little harder with you. You were only eight years old the last time I saw you, you know."

With the others, it was not hard at all.

Mama had looked the same all her life. She had been a short, plump woman with dark hair combed back into a simple bun. As a Defenseless Mennonite Mama had been very strict about dress: dark dresses, a black veil over her hair, and when she went out of the house, a black bonnet.

In spite of her somber appearance, Mama had been a happy person. She had known how to laugh and to sing—she always sang at her work—and the joy of the Lord had been a glow of sunshine radiating from the inner part of her being.

Some of all that had somehow carried over into her new life, and now that Louisa saw her again, it was not at all hard to recognize Mama.

Papa had been a young man when he came from Switzerland about the time of the Civil War. All of the time Louisa had known him, he had been a bearded man who dressed in black. It was not hard to recognize Papa, either.

Or Mabel, Louisa's daughter-in-law.

"Oh, wonderful!" Louisa spoke the words with laughter in her cracking voice and clung to the syllables as if she were reluctant to part with a word that was, in itself, somehow wonderful. Deep peace welled up from within her and spread across her face while a soft smile rested there, as though it had come home where it belonged.

"Wonderful," she said again, and both hands reached out, as if to touch the vision.

In whispered consultation with the watchers by her bed, Louisa rejoiced. "I'm going *home,*" she said to them. "That's what this means, isn't it?" She drew in her breath suddenly, like a delighted child. "I'm going *home* today!"

Louisa was not left alone with her vision. In the other bed, her roommate stirred into wakefulness, and an aide came just in time to catch the last of Louisa's words.

The aide stopped for a moment to stare at Louisa with pursed lips. "Funny old woman," she mumbled, shaking her head. The look on her face said, "This one has *always* been old."

The aide was one who meant to be kind. She took adequate care of the residents who were assigned to her. She often said that she loved the old people she cared for—and she believed it.

Fanny, the aide, never looked any of her charges squarely in the eye, as if she believed that they were real people who could meet her look. Fanny's nostrils flared to say plainly, "Old people stink—all of them."

Fanny thought she was being kind when she marched into the room with a hearty "Good morning, girls!" and shoved a cold bedpan in with Louisa.

Louisa tore herself away from her spiritual visitors long enough to try to straighten the blanket again to cover herself but it was hard—she was so very weak—and she couldn't manage the task.

Even her weakness was a reminder of what day it was. She smiled at it and went back to her rejoicing.

From her first moment of awareness, a single thought had come to Louisa. "I'm going to see *him!* I'm going to see *Jesus.*"

Glad tears came to her eyes. "After ninety years of walking in faith, I am going to see him at last!"

This delight pressed in upon her until that single thought was all that mattered.

Meanwhile, the aide went around the room, bringing fresh water, taking care of waste paper, and making all the hopeful, comforting noises she thought an aide was supposed to make.

She helped Louisa's roommate get up and dressed and on the way to the dining room for breakfast.

"She's talking about going home again," the roommate, Rosie, whispered to Fanny, when the aide leaned close to lift her from the bed.

"I know, dear," said Fanny. "It's all right."

"It is *not* all right!" shrieked Rosie. "She's not supposed to *do* that. Her son Wallace said she shouldn't. She's supposed to keep quiet and get used to being here, like the rest of us. She's not going home. Not ever again!"

Rosie's sharp tone was loud enough that a few of her words penetrated Louisa's thoughts and demanded her attention.

"But I *am*," she protested softly. "I *am* going home. I'm going *today.*"

"Now, Mrs. B.," said Fanny. "We know better than that, don't we?" She settled Rosie into a wheelchair and started out the door with her.

"Call my son," Louisa said, her voice thin and quavering. "Call Wallace. Tell him what I said. This is *the day,* and I'm going home. Wallace will understand."

She hoped that Wallace would understand. Whether he understood or not, she was going anyway.

Louisa turned back to her visitors. There were things she wanted to ask them.

She became so absorbed in her questions that nurse Jensen's entrance startled her.

"GOOD MORNING, LOUISA," she said as she entered. She spoke loudly, hoping that Louisa would hear her words and because of the loudness her voice sounded gruff. Her eyes were gentle and loving—concerned for Louisa. "FANNY SAYS YOU ARE TALKING ABOUT GOING HOME AGAIN."

Louisa looked at her, closed her eyes, then looked again, as if she were finding her way back to the room from a great distance. "Yes," she said, nodding. Enough of the nurse's words had been heard. "Yes. I'll be leaving today."

A look of sadness came to Mrs. Jensen then. Louisa seemed like her old self again, and that was good. The thought of watching the old woman fight her old battle with homesickness troubled the nurse. She held the wrinkled hand in her own comfortingly. Her eyes searched Louisa's. "You know you CAN'T DO THAT," she said. "You need us to take care of you."

The nurse's face and voice showed no comprehension of what Louisa had said.

"You don't understand." The words bore more than just a thin coating of chagrin. "I'm going *home!*"

If she had only said, "I'm dying," they might have understood. But that which was happening to Louisa—the joy, the peace, the reunion with family and friends—was so far removed from death as it was usually understood that she never thought to call it that. And no one thought to grasp her deeper meaning.

Mrs. Jensen stood there, wanting to help, but feeling helpless. When the silence became awkward, she patted Louisa's hand and turned to leave.

"Please," Louisa quavered after her. "Please! Tell my son. If you don't believe me, at least tell my son what I said."

The nurse turned back and studied Louisa for a long moment. Perhaps there was something in the old woman's face . . . .

Mrs. Jensen, shrugging her shoulders, agreed. "ALL RIGHT. I'll call him. Is there ANYTHING ELSE you want me to TELL HIM?"

"Yes." Louisa smiled deep gratitude. "Tell him to bring Gayle with him when he comes. I've got to talk to Gayle before I go."

There was one other thing that Louisa needed to do, but at that moment she was too tired. It would have to wait until after she had rested.

The conversation, the awareness of this special time, even the joy—they were all tiring.

The nurse gone, Louisa sank back onto the pillow and closed her eyes for a brief nap. She would take care of that other matter after she had rested.

16

THIS I WAS, THIS I AM

The clatter and clank of the breakfast cart came down the hall. An aide entered with a tray to end Louisa's brief nap.

"Here you go, Mrs. B. Oatmeal . . . buttered toast . . . stewed prunes . . . a poached egg . . . and a pot of tea." The aide uncovered each item with a flourish as she named it. "Doesn't that look *good?*"

Inwardly, Louisa shook her head. Hearing one word was enough for her to guess the rest, but she had never been able to convince herself that those morning trays of cold food looked particularly good. Now that she was going home, there was no need to pretend.

"No," she said. "It doesn't."

The aide looked at her with a half-frown, half-surprised smile. Recovering, she went on with the morning routine.

"Here . . . I'll crank your bed up a little. Do you want me to *help* you *eat* this morning?"

"No, thank you," said Louisa, who had no intention of wasting time on something so earthly as food, when all of her attention had already gone homeward. "I can feed myself all I want . . . . But would you hand me my tablet and a pencil from the drawer?"

The aide put the requested items on top of the nightstand. She shook her head, knowing Louisa could neither feed herself nor write. "Good luck," she said as she left to deliver other trays. "I'll check back in on you pretty soon, to be sure you're doing all right," she promised.

Louisa—breakfast and aide quickly forgotten in the urgency of the work that needed to be done—picked up her tablet. With trembling hands that sometimes slipped as though they had forgotten what she ordered them to do, Louisa turned the pages.

She had to check and make certain that the important pages were still there, the instructions that her family—children, grandchildren, and great-greats—would need tomorrow.

Obituary, said the straggling black letters at the top of the page she was looking for, and then, *Louisa Nussbaum. I was born in Bluffton, Ohio, in the year of 1869. March 28 . . .*

The writing had been a great struggle for Louisa. She had finished it months ago when she could still make a pencil move almost legibly across a piece of paper. She hadn't written it by sentences or even words, but letter by slow, painful letter.

. . . I was converted at the age of sixteen in 1886, and joined the Defenseless Church, and later joined the Missionary Church . . . .

I love my Lord so much. He is my life, my everything. Could I ever part from Thee? No. Never. A thousand times, no!

Louisa's eyes had closed again, and her fingers were resting from their search when the breakfast aide came back into the room.

"Oh, Mrs. B!" scolded the aide as she entered.

Louisa struggled through waves of dream-filled drowsiness to the right place and the right time.

"You haven't eaten a *thing,*" the aide went on. "Not one bite!"

Why in the world, wondered Louisa, *do I hear them so much better when they scold?*

"Here," Louisa said. She held the tablet toward the aide. "Find it for me."

It took a small eternity of repititions—"obituary . . . o . . . bit . . . u . . . ary . . . find the page that says *obituary*" before Louisa communicated what she wanted.

The breakfast aide flipped through the tablet with agile fingers and handed it back to Louisa. "There you go," she said.

Louisa took the open tablet, wrapped her arms around it, and held it to her heart.

The aide had the morning mail with her this time, and she opened Louisa's two letters and read them to her—very loudly. There was a card—"Thinking of you"—from one of her great granddaughters and a letter from Wallace.

It would have been nice, thought Louisa, *if I could have read them myself just this one last time.* She smiled wryly. *It would have been nice if I could even have heard all the words when she read them. They are the last letters I'll ever get in this world, after all.*

But she could not, and there was really no sense feeling sad over that. Listening carefully, she took in those words she could catch as food for her soul.

She refused food for her body, although the aide kept trying to force her to eat. As she read Louisa's letters, she kept dipping the spoon into cereal, egg, whatever, and offering it to her.

At each spoonful Louisa shook her head and clamped her lips shut. "I'm going home today," she whispered a gentle reminder to herself. "I don't need that kind of food. It's my soul and spirit that need to be strong now."

Letters finished, the aide left with the breakfast tray, still scolding. "I don't know how you expect to get your strength back, Mrs. B., if you won't eat. I just don't know . . . ." Shaking her head and mumbling, she was gone.

Louisa smiled at the gentle tirade, some of which she could almost hear, and went back to her tablet. Now that she had found the place, she knew what was written there. It was as if she could see the words. She had written down her life for them—the most important things that she wanted them to remember about her.

I was married to A.L. Hochstetler on May 23, 1889.

While Louisa paused to think about Amos, Rosie came back. There was no aide with her. She came under her own wobbly power, working her wheelchair through the door in awkward fashion, catching it on one side, then the other, and—at last—safely through.

Louisa turned again to her tablet, letting her fingers run back and forth across it as if she could absorb the straggling words through them.

There was a sudden, loud, and very distracting commotion in the hall. "Cora! Don't do that! No, Cora!" But the shout was too late. "Oh, shoot!" The voice was followed almost immediately by a raucous buzzing and the pounding of footsteps. Cora had opened the emergency door again.

Hurrying aides closed the door, recaptured Cora, and escorted her back down the hallway.

Back and forth went Louisa's finger.

I was left alone in the darkness with my babies. There wasn't any light. Yes, many dark hours passed and were gone, but God was with me even in that awful darkness.

Before I was married again, there were many hardships. At times we had hardly anything to eat, and I often sent the children to bed hungry. That should never have been necessary. It was a matter of neglect. There was plenty of food in existence.

Louisa never lied to anybody about those dark hours and the fact that she was a divorced woman, but she never volunteered the information, either. It was a dark chapter in her life. It remained dark until she died.

Two more aides came then to interrupt Louisa and change her bed.

Roll the old woman over to one side. Get that tablet out of the way. That can't be important. She's senile anyhow. Nothing she wrote could be important.

Get the old woman out of the way. Put a clean bottom sheet on that side of the bed.

Roll the old woman over to the other side. Get her out of the way. Pull the clean sheet over that side of the bed, too.

Talk back and forth while you work, otherwise you might have to notice that the old woman is a person, not a thing.

"Did you stay up and watch that movie on TV last night?"

"Yeah. And boy, am I tired!"

"Move your elbow, Mrs. B."

"My kids threw a fit because I didn't let them stay up."

"I never told mine about it. They can't read yet, so I was safe."

"Cover her legs there when we get her moved."

"Why, for Pete's sake? She don't know the difference."

Shrug your shoulders, smooth the blanket, and leave.

Louisa did know the difference. They couldn't hurt her now, not on the day she was going home. She was glad, though, to see them leave with their stack of sheets and blankets for the next room.

Once they quit poking and jostling and rolling her over, she could reach out to the nightstand for her tablet and go back to her memories.

In 1919, when I was fifty years old, my heavenly Father sent Christian Basinger to me, and we were married in late July—or was it early August?—of that year.

They had had a good life together, and a long one, all things considered. God had blessed their marriage. Chris had provided well for Louisa and she loved him.

Louisa paused to think about Chris for a moment; then she stared down at the next words on her tablet. *My aim in life was to help others.*

"What is that in thine hand?" God asked Moses out of the burning bush.

Moses answered, "A rod."

God used that rod to deliver the people of faith.

If God had asked Louisa the same question, she might well have answered, "Well . . . uh . . . it's a jar of pickles, Lord."

That, too, in the hand of a woman like Louisa, could minister to people.

Money was not what Louisa had used to help others. She never had much in the way of material goods.

She helped with things like homemade jams and jellies and dill pickles and quilts.

She helped others by giving herself in love.

The summer that she was ninety-one, Louisa canned over two hundred quarts of fruit and vegetables. She also made relishes, jelly, and several varieties of pickles.

By that age, of course, she was slowing down and wasn't able to do as much as she had when younger.

But every summer until Wallace and Mary came to take her to the nursing home, she canned the harvest of their garden.

It wasn't just for herself and Chris, either. There was the
Bible school in Ft. Wayne, Indiana, supported by the Missionary
Church. Each year for many years, Louisa sent a share of her can-
ning to the students there. And of course she shared with
friends around Pandora.

The summer that Hattie Miller was sick and unable to
plant her garden, Louisa organized the neighbor women to can
some things for the Millers.

"Come on over to the house," she said to her friends when
cherries were ripe, "and bring along any extra cherries you got.
We'll spend the day together. I'll fix us a little lunch, and we'll
put up those cherries.

"Hattie and Ben can use them, what with those six kids,
and her sick and all."

Louisa did the same thing again when tomatoes were ripe,
and corn, green beans, and peaches.

That was the summer she was ninety-five.

At the time her eyes weakened to the point where she had
to give up quilting, Louisa had been at it for over fifty years. She
had made well over a hundred quilts. How much over, she
couldn't remember, a combination of growing a little absent-
minded, and losing count.

Many of the quilts were sent to foreign countries to be
used by missionaries in the field.

One of Louisa's most prized possessions was a letter
from a missionary in Africa:

Dear friend,

I feel that I must write and tell you what happened to
the beautiful quilt you gave us when we were last home
on furlough.

I hope you will not be angry. And please don't feel—
because of the way we used the quilt—that we did not
value it.

About ten days ago one of our dear friends here fell ill
of fever and died.

There is not much in the way of trees hereabouts, so
we had no lumber for a coffin, and we had no proper way
to bury her.

We used your quilt.

Please understand . . .

"Actually," said Louisa, when she told the story later, "I felt quite honored to think my quilt was fine enough for that purpose." A true quilter, she always took great care and pride in her work, especially the quilts destined for the mission field.

In the winter of 1959, when she was only ninety, Louisa made two quilts, one an Ohio Star pattern and the other a Dutch windmill. She had planned to give the Dutch windmill to a missionary family she knew.

"But," she sighed, slightly embarrassed, "I made a few bad stitches, so it isn't good enough." She nodded agreement with herself. "I have to have a perfect one to give to missionaries."

The weight of the writing pad was tiring Louisa. Although she was not in pain, she felt inexpressibly weary, as though all the tiredness of her entire life were pressing down on her. She was ready to rest.

It was becoming somewhat difficult to breathe.

Louisa, struggling, turned one more page. That was where the rest of it should be.

Songs at the church, it should say. *"Beyond the Sunset" and "Beautiful Garden." Helen to sing.* Louisa had loved those hymns all her life. They would do well as an accompaniment to her departure. No one had ever sung them quite like Helen Groshong, it seemed to her.

At the grave, sing "I'll Meet You in the Morning." Pastor David Eby and Pastor Thomas Smyth to officiate. Please and thank you all children, singers and pastors. My aim in life was to help others . . . .

The words, the last ones Louisa had ever written, dwindled away, almost illegibly, at the bottom of the page. Remembering, she could feel again the dismay that had filled her when it happened, and she knew that she might never be able to write again.

There was something more now that she wanted to add. Just two words, she needed to put them there . . . her last written words in this world should be grateful ones.

Louisa reached for the pencil on her night stand. "Thank you," she wanted to write.

"Please, God," she whispered. "Please, dear Friend, help me to do it."

Louisa touched the point of her pencil to the paper and nothing showed but some very light straggling lines. Her words of gratitude would never be written.

The great weariness took over Louisa's hands at last, as it had done the rest of her body. Sighing, she felt the pencil and the tablet slip from her fingers. The pencil rolled until it dropped and landed with a soft, wooden thud on the floor beneath the bed.

"Oh well," said Louisa to her God. "I love you, anyhow."

The tablet slid a few inches down the slight hill her body made beneath the sheet, then stopped, open, on the edge of the bed, where Wallace would see it when he came. Louisa did not have the energy to retrieve it.

She turned again to the old friends at her bedside, the ones no one else could see. "It's all there," she told them, fluttering her fingers toward the tablet.

Her eyes closed.

The morning sun had moved from the bed, across the room to the dresser. Louisa lay motionless in soft shadow, dreaming no more of the past, but of the precious, promised experience that lay ahead of her.

Louisa dozed for a while and awoke worried.

Although there was a clock on her roommate's bedside table, it was too far away for Louisa to see the time. The sun had narrowed to a thin strip at the left of the window, and it soon would be gone behind the point of roof outside. An aide had placed a lunch tray on Louisa's bed table while she drowsed. It must be some time after noon.

Wallace should have been there.

And Gayle.

Louisa's wandering thoughts halted. "Stop a while here," she told them. "I love that young man."

That in itself was not so unusual. Louisa had much love to give. She had cared for a lot of people in her lifetime.

Even at that, Gayle was special.

Sometimes, just for fun, Louisa tried to imagine what he might have been like when he was a boy—before she knew him. In her imagination there was a picture of a barefoot, freckle-faced youngster—tow-headed beneath the summer sun—with jug-handle ears and small for his age, but strong. He wore rolled-up overalls and a shirt with a hole in it. That little boy never started a fight—but he could usually finish one. He had courage and stood up for himself. There were some who called him "that Harkins roughneck!"

Actually, Louisa had not met Gayle until the day she began to pray for him. He was a young man then. Norma brought him to Louisa to introduce him. They had just been married.

She had liked her granddaughter's handsome, smiling husband from the beginning, although he hadn't yet learned to know God.

"That's all right for women and older folks, Gramma," he said to her once, "but a man has to learn to rely on himself."

Louisa prayed for him, worried about him a little bit, and fussed over him.

Gayle changed his mind, though. "You were right, Gramma," he said, a little embarrassed by the admission. "God's not just for women and old people. I need him, too."

Her habit of praying, worrying, and fussing were well established, and Louisa kept on with it, even after she knew Gayle had made everything right between himself and God.

As she lay dying, one of the things she wanted most was to see Gayle once more before she left, and tell him just once more . . . .

A sound at the door interrupted her thoughts, and she cried out the names of the two persons most in her mind.

"Wallace?"

"Gayle?"

It was her doctor who crossed to the bed and looked down at her.

"It's not your son, Louisa," he said. "It's only me."

"Oh." The small, insignificant word was filled with disappointment.

"Did they send for him? Wallace? Did they call my boy?" Pain pounded in Louisa's chest, as though given strength by her anxiety. It was hard, for the moment, to talk around the hurting. Her eyes held the doctor's, and there was pain there, too. It spilled over into her voice.

"I wanted him to come. I know he wants to say good-by before I go."

"Yes," said the doctor, speaking emphatically for Louisa's benefit. "They gave him your message, and he's on his way."

Louisa smiled then, catching just enough of his words to answer her frightened questions, and the chest pain, born of her longing and anxiety, went away.

"I wonder they didn't tell me," she said.

"I wonder, too," said the doctor, with a thin edge of irritation in his voice. He thought that it was a pity that one of those aides couldn't have walked down the hall to her with the message from her son.

Louisa was his oldest patient. He both admired her and enjoyed her. She was a plain-spoken old woman. When she thought somebody was wrong, she said so. But when she thought they were right, she said that, too.

It was unusual to say that someone so old could be beautiful—but there was an undeniable beauty about Louisa. And a serenity of spirit that he hadn't seen in many others.

He nodded at the tray on her table. "You haven't eaten your lunch."

"I was sleeping when they brought it," she replied. She hated to admit that. Even on her last day, there was something about sleeping when the sun was up that bothered her.

The doctor picked up a spoon and offered Louisa a bite of red jello. She took that bite only to please him.

Then she turned her head. "Please . . . don't make me eat it. Sometimes the aides make me eat, but I really don't want to now." There was so much pathos in the words and in her eyes that he found himself having a most undoctor-like reaction.

He frowned, put the spoon down and carried the tray into the hall.

"There," he said, when he came back. "Now nobody will make you eat if you don't want to."

He leaned down and propped his forearms on the bed rail as he held Louisa's hand and brushed the straggling hair back from her face. He always did that when he was with her. This might be the last time. Unless he was reading his charts wrong, the old woman was dying. After 106 years, her body had worn out.

He would miss her.

As if she had read his mind, Louisa interrupted his thoughts. "Someone else will be your oldest patient soon."

"Now, Louisa," he said, straightening. "You shouldn't talk like that."

"Why not? It's true." Her faded blue eyes shone with an inner light. "I'm going home."

His puzzled frown reminded her that she shouldn't say it like that—that people didn't understand. So she said it the other way in explanation.

"I'm dying." The change in words didn't make any difference. The inner light was still there.

He had never talked to his patients about their dying.

"Oh, come on, Louisa. You've got a few more good years in you yet."

Louisa wouldn't let him avoid the subject. "Pshaw!" she said. "I'm 106 years old, and I know what I know."

Speaking of her death brought the worry back, and she couldn't help fussing about it a little. "Where's Wallace?"

"He'll be here any minute, now. It takes time to drive over from Mansfield, you know."

The doctor was silent, then, looking into the face of his patient. "This," he thought, "is some kind of woman." There was a knot in his throat, and he tried to swallow around it. He felt tears that he refused to shed. He wondered at the power of a worn-out old woman to touch him so.

He should have gone. There were other patients in his office waiting for him, and his office staff would wonder what was taking so long. But he hated to leave her at this final good-by. In some way he could not understand, he drew from the feeble hand he held a strength that would last him the rest of his life.

Louisa reached up and patted his arm to comfort him. He never knew that in that moment Louisa Basinger prayed for him.

There came sounds from the hallway: hurried footsteps, the whisper of fabric against fabric as someone pulled off a coat as they walked, and the rapid breathing that went with walking fast.

Wallace and Mary burst through the door. The doctor turned to business again.

After the first flurry of greetings, the doctor called Wallace aside for a quiet conversation—too low for Louisa to hear.

"She could very well be right," he said. "She could go any time . . . or it could be several days yet."

Their attempt to hide their conversation irritated Louisa. They didn't need to think she didn't know what they were talking about.

Young people were so foolish. Sometimes they acted— just because she was old—as if she couldn't figure out what was going on any more.

"Mama," said Mary, bending over the bed. "They called us. They said . . . ." She didn't continue. She seemed upset.

So foolish . . . .

"Don't be upset about it," Louisa said. "I'm going home today. That's all. I'm just going home."

She whispered the story of what had happened to her that day—how she woke to find old friends, long dead, at her bedside and had realized what day it was.

"Are they still there, Mama?" Mary looked pale when she spoke. She glanced around the room as if searching for specters.

"Oh, yes. They're just . . . waiting."

She told them how she had tried to explain to the nurses, aides, and her roommate, but none of them seemed to understand.

"I've this for you." Louisa's fingers found the tablet teetering on the edge of the bed. "You'll need it tomorrow."

"It's for the obituary . . . and about the funeral and all."

Mary's eyes were wide in horror. Without looking at the pages, she ripped them out of the tablet and shoved them into her purse.

So foolish . . . .

Across the room, the doctor put a hand on Wallace's shoulder. "It's just a matter of time now," he said. "Only God knows how much." He turned toward the bed. "Good-by, Louisa. Good-by, my friend."

Wallace came back to stand beside Louisa's bed.

Louisa sighed in contentment. If Gayle would only come.

They sat holding hands, the three of them, in a circle—as they had done around the table when Wallace and Mary were children. For a brief moment it seemed to Louisa that Jacob and Oliver were there, too. There was a checkered oilcloth with homemade bread and butter and fresh strawberries. The long-ago, adolescent voice of Wallace was saying, "Thank you, Father, for food and family . . . ," while the rest of the family echoed, "Amen."

As they sat there, silent, cherishing each other, the moment of closeness, and their memories, Louisa said something she hadn't expected to say.

It might hurt them; nobody had admitted, after all, that there might be something to forgive. Louisa tried to be careful with her words—but it had to be said before she went from them. If it weren't, they would wonder, later.

"I've forgiven you, you know, for making me come and live here."

It was just as well that she couldn't see them clearly. Anger flashed in Mary's eyes, as if someone had struck flint and steel there. The muscles along Wallace's jaw worked briefly, and his eyes closed, as if to hide what could be read in them.

Her children sat stiff and silent in their anger, and then, as suddenly as it had come, it was gone.

Perhaps the circumstances made the difference. Before, they had tried to ignore her anger with them.

Now the words had been said, and they had to accept them. And if they weren't going to let her go from them with feelings of anger between them, they, too, had to forgive.

"That's . . . that's good to know, Ma," Wallace said. His voice reflected emotion, but it wasn't anger. No, definitely it was not anger.

Five minutes later, more of Louisa's family came. There were a couple of grandchildren, and two or three of the great-grandchildren, as well.

Finally, Gayle followed Norma through the door. Like a messenger sent to announce some great event, he came. The time was at hand.

17

AND THE CHILDREN CRIED

There were six of Louisa's descendants present at her dying—and Gayle, the one she had often wished were more hers than through marriage.

They scattered themselves sadly about the room, waiting for the release that she was waiting for, although they felt differently about it.

Louisa spoke briefly with the unseen watchers by her bed. "It will be soon, now, won't it? . . . I can tell them it will be soon? . . . I don't like to see them have to wait here long . . . It's hard for them."

The answer she received apparently satisfied her. She realized that she felt chilly, and asked for a blanket, which someone brought. Then she snuggled under the covers, warm, contented, smiling and happy, to wait with them.

The children on the other hand—Louisa thought of all of her descendants as children—all of the children cried.

It wasn't death that made them cry. None of them were afraid of that. One of the greatest blessings God gave to Louisa was that her children knew him in the same personal, friendly way that she did.

They weren't crying for Louisa, either, because they knew the joy that was waiting for her.

But there were memories in that room—and there was so much love.

When a person who is loved leaves, there is always an empty place and loneliness. When that leaving is death, there is such finality. They missed her already. So they wept in anticipation of the empty place she would leave.

The memories, too, brought tears. All of them remembered what had been—and would never be again.

Wallace was still beside her bed, although the three of them stopped holding hands to welcome the others.

Standing there, he remembered the time she had whipped him for fighting with Jacob. What had started that? He didn't know anymore.

It was a summertime fight. The sun was hot, but the clouds had just disappeared after one of those heavy, Ohio summer downpours. There was slippery mud under the grass in the back yard.

They had been scuffling, and both of them were muddy and wet. Wallace was getting the best of the fight, but Jacob had hit some good licks, too. Wallace's nose was bleeding, and his arm was full of slivers from one of the wooden fence posts.

Really angry by that time, Wallace dragged Jacob into the outhouse and tried to stuff him, head first, through the biggest hole in the plank seat.

Jacob's yells, added to the general racket they were creating, brought Ma running from cleaning one of the upstairs bedrooms. She still held a dust rag in her hand.

Wallace never found out whether Jacob would have fit through that hole.

Ma had collared them—both almost as big as she was—and dragged them back out into the yard by the scruff of their necks, like an angry mother cat with two naughty kittens.

She held them that way until they calmed down. Then she borrowed Wallace's belt and whipped them.

"Funny thing to be remembering at a time like this," he thought.

"Or maybe not so funny. It was typical of Ma, her strength—typical, too, of the way she had of seeing what ought to be done and doing it."

He hadn't seen her often in weak moments.

Once, though. Just after the divorce, when she had taken Wallace, Jacob, and Mary back to Pandora, she fell down the splintery wood steps of their back porch carrying a huge basket of wet laundry. She landed hard on the rocky path at the bottom of the steps. Her knees and the palms of her hands were cut, scraped, and bruised.

She didn't say anything except, "Ouch!" She certainly didn't cry—not until after Wallace had heard the sound of her fall and had come racing around the corner of the house. He stopped suddenly, as if he had bumped into a brick wall at full speed. As soon as he saw what had happened, he ran to kneel in the dirt beside her and put his arms around her.

"Oh, Mama!" he said. "Mama . . . Mama!"

There were tears in young Wallace's eyes.

Then Ma cried. It was not from pain—cuts, scrapes, and bruises were all forgotten—but from relief.

"Oh, Wallace," she said, "I thought you were so mad you couldn't even love me anymore." She buried her head on his strong young shoulder and held on.

He shook his head, remembering. How could she ever have thought *that?*

"I love you, Ma," he whispered to the tired, shriveled, old woman in the bed. "I always have."

Mary's thoughts were wandering too—racing off down worn, dusty roads into the past to touch childhood's treasures she had left there.

Mama . . . with wisps of prematurely white hair straggling into her eyes, bending to pull loaves of hot bread from the oven . . . rubbing butter into the crust to keep it soft . . . pretending to fight off young, eager hands that reached out, begging for a slice still hot . . . cooking fresh garden vegetables in those days when hot bread and vegetables from their own garden were all they had to put on their table . . . making a cobbler of wild blackberries sweetened with soda, because there was no money for sugar.

Mama . . . angry with Papa in the days when he had first left them . . . so hurt, and so human as she paced the kitchen floor in rage and humiliation, speaking aloud all the things she felt against him. She had gone to them one at a time after that, telling them, "I'm sorry. He's your Papa and I loved him once.

"Whatever happens, that much will always be true. I had no right to let you hear me talk against him like that."

Mama . . . spending long hours by Mary's bedside when she was sick . . . holding her head when she needed to vomit into a bucket. "The rest of you children stay out of there," Mama would say then. "Mary is sick, and I want you to keep away from her, so you don't come down with whatever she's got."

Mama . . . growing older and more set in her ways.

Wallace and Mary had gone one summer Sunday afternoon to take Mama and Chris for a drive. They drove to Bluffton, then over to Mt. Cory, before they turned west—back to Pandora. With the turns they made, back and forth and around the rich Ohio farmland, directions for their passengers became a bit confused. Louisa was adamant they were headed north when they turned west toward Pandora.

Old fashioned things like the position of the sun and directions didn't ordinarily bother Mama much, though.

It was the new gadgets like television that were more likely to disturb her.

She never understood television at all.

For one thing, she was almost 85 years old the first time she saw one.

For another, she had never seen a motion picture in a theater. The Missionary Church did not approve of them; therefore, Mama didn't approve of them either.

She had seen home movies, though. Somebody had given Wallace a movie camera, and he took pictures everywhere he went. He brought them to the house on Monroe Street to show them to her and Chris, and they were fascinating, almost like a family reunion.

Mama did enjoy those home movies—real people whom she knew, waving at her from the shiny, white screen Wallace set up in the front room.

It seemed logical to Mama, when she first saw a television set, that those were real people, too—what they were doing was real.

"I just don't understand," Mama would say, squinting across at the little black and white screen, "How they can let somebody make pictures of them like that—and show the whole country how they're living."

The grandchildren and the great-grandchildren would howl with laughter at that. "Gramma, those are *actors*. They aren't really doing those things," they would explain.

But nobody ever convinced her. Mama was always a woman who knew what she knew.

"Thank you, Mama," whispered Mary—she was thinking of something other than television—"for sticking by what you knew."

Around the room, the grandchildren, too, worked through their memories—of visits to Louisa's house during vacations and holidays.

Geraldine, for a reason that she couldn't understand, remembered things more than incidents. She thought of the roller skates Gramma kept in the basement for the children to use, and the sidewalk with grass-filled cracks that always tripped them up when they skated.

She remembered a banana popsicle Gramma got for her one Friday afternoon at the grocery—and how sick the popsicle made her, ruining the entire week-end visit.

She remembered red strawberry jam on a white crocheted antimacassar. She had been leaning over the back of a tall, sturdy, stuffed armchair to look out the window while she ate fresh bread spread thick with homemade butter and jam.

The jam betrayed her, dribbling off the bread onto the crocheted pineapples of the antimacassar. Gramma had told her not to eat in the front room, too!

Geraldine tried to hide the jam by turning the antimacassar around, so that the jam was hidden behind the chair. Then she pinned it down again.

The only problem was that as soon as Gramma came into the room, she gave the chair a funny look and said, "Now how did those pineapples get upside down? Geraldine?

Gramma turned the antimacassar around and found the jam.

No . . . she remembered events that had happened, too.

When they were very small and had come for a visit, Gramma would tell them bedtime stories from the Bible. But when they got a little older, she did something different when it was time to tuck them in. Gramma would say a Bible verse, then Geraldine would say one, then Gramma, and so on, until Geraldine fell asleep, and Gramma could slip down the stairs to her own room.

There was the night Geraldine was in Pandora with her cousin, Marjorie, and they were so giggly and noisy at bedtime.

Gramma had tucked them in and said Bible verses, but none of it had done much good. The two of them went on and on, chattering and laughing and making strange thumpings on the floor, until Gramma came to the foot of the stairs in her pink flannel nightgown to call up to them, "Why can't you girls be quiet and go to sleep?"

There was never a good answer to a question like that in Gramma's house. They didn't even try to find a good answer.

"Tell her we can't find the bed," Geraldine whispered to Marjorie.

"Huh! You tell her," Marjorie whispered back.

"OK . . . Because we can't find the be-e-e-e-ed!" called Geraldine.

There was a long silence at the bottom of the stairs. "Geraldine!" said Gramma. "Marjorie!"

They quickly were quiet and asleep.

Even in the midst of sadness and tears, Geraldine could smile while she relived those moments. She had fine memories.

She went to the side of her Gramma's bed and leaned down to take her hand. The ancient eyes fluttered open and brightened when they saw who it was.

"Gramma," said the granddaughter, "I'm going now." The knuckles of her other hand were white on the railing. Geraldine felt like breaking down and crying and taking Gramma in her arms to hold her until she died. She recognized her feeling but fought it.

"I never have liked good-bys, Gramma," she said. "So I'll just say so long for a while. I'll see you later. I hope it won't be too long."

Louisa didn't hear any of the choked words, but she seemed to understand. With one finger she reached out and briefly touched the clenched hand on the railing.

Geraldine picked up her purse, turned, and slowly walked away.

Auf Wiedersehen, Louisa whispered after her.

Auf Wiedersehen, Geraldine stopped to whisper back.

Geraldine wouldn't go to the funeral, either. "Gramma's not dead," she said when they asked her why. "I can't go to the celebration of a dead body. That's not my Gramma."

Over in a corner away from the bed, Norma held Gayle's hand and watched Geraldine leave.

"I couldn't just leave like that," she said. "I've got to have every minute with her I can get. I had such a little . . . ." The words faded and were lost in thoughts that never made it to her lips.

" . . . such a little dab of memories, anyhow," she thought. "I didn't get to see much of Gramma—not even when I was growing up. She was much closer to Aunt Mary's children, because they lived so close—and I was so far away."

How she wished it might have been otherwise! For a moment, envy of her cousins stabbed at Norma's heart. She could have cried for what they had had—and what she had missed.

That wasn't right, either. Those same cousins had contributed so much to what memories there were.

"We really did have a good time together," she thought.

Whenever Norma went to Gramma's house for a week or so, the cousins were usually there, too.

They would all go over to Main Street on Saturday night—that was the entertainment of the week in the little farm community—and admire the handsome country boys.

Norma was a different person in Pandora than she was at home. Her cousins had thought that she was a sophisticated city girl.

"Actually," she thought, "I was more naive and protected than all the rest of them put together."

Gramma always kept a protective eye on them, though.

A dark-haired girl who lived near Gramma got pregnant and Gramma would point the girl out to her granddaughters. She would caution them about ending up like "that girl." Norma, for a long time after that warning, was afraid even to kiss her boyfriends.

Gramma's watchfulness had made her seem like a stern, unbending woman. The cousins had talked about it among themselves during some of those summer vacations. They were never able to understand it—not until later, when they had children and grandchildren of their own.

If taking good care of them had delighted Gramma, so did finding little, special things to do for them.

She always had hickory nuts in her pantry, and the cousins would dip them into a small dish of salt. It was one of their favorite snacks.

Gramma would make apple dumplings for them, too. Unlike other grandmothers, Louisa was not one of the world's great cooks. By closing her eyes and concentrating, Norma could almost taste the crust on those dumplings again.

Ugh! It was terrible!

But as her grandchildren, they had somehow understood—and loved—the love behind it all, and they had eaten the results of Gramma's cooking in the spirit in which it was offered.

In the basement of the house on Monroe Street, Gramma always had row after row of canned fruits and vegetables. She would let them go down and pick their own favorite kind of fruit to serve with her meals.

The problem was that the cobwebbed basement was so dark and scary that when it was Norma's turn, she would grab the first jar of fruit she came to and run back up the stairs.

One time pigtailed Norma crept down the stairs with her hand on the rough stone wall for balance. As she reached the bottom, she thought she heard a noise, and she grabbed a jar, hurrying back up the stairs and through the door to safety.

"Here, Gramma," she said, and handed Louisa the jar she had chosen.

Gramma looked at the jar, then at Norma, then back at the jar again. "This," she asked, "is your favorite fruit?" She held the glass container out for Norma to see.

It was a jar of green beans.

Norma trudged back to the deep, dark basement to trade it for peaches.

Gramma had done some funny things, too. The old woman knew how to be just a bit cantankerous at times—at the table, for example, when she would scold Chris for making so much noise with his false teeth while he ate. The grandchildren or the great-grandchildren gathered around them would just grin—along with Chris's big, patient grin—because Gramma would be making the same noise with her own teeth.

Norma sighed, and from the bed came another kind of sigh, as Louisa's breathing became heavier, more labored.

It was Norma's turn to cross to the bed. "How are you feeling, Gramma?" she asked.

There was no answer, only a nod and the slight smile that Louisa's strength could afford.

"So few memories," Norma thought again, *"we have until we see you again."*

"Lord God," she prayed in the silent places of her heart, "this was a woman among women. You really did something fine in this life."

Norma, too, whispered her farewell. "I love you, Gramma. I enjoyed knowing you. And I'm proud to be one of your descendants."

In room 34 at Parmenter County Nursing Home, they all whispered their final, sad words to Louisa around their tears . . . . .

. . . while Louisa whispered love back to them and began, smiling softly, to use the last of her breath and strength in singing an old hymn.

18

LOUISA GOES HOME

The others looked at Louisa in surprise.

Singing?

Wallace bent over her, his ear to her lips to catch the words she was barely able to utter.

Her voice was cracked and weak. It faded in and out, so that there were words that even Wallace missed, as close to her as he was. The tune was hardly there at all.

Louisa, lying there with her eyes closed—pale and still at the threshold of death—was definitely singing.

"Lead, kindly Light . . . amid . . . th'en . . . circling . . . gloom.
Lead Thou . . . me . . . on . . . .
The morn . . . ing . . . dawns . . . "

She had changed the words! "Listen!" said Wallace, looking up at them suddenly. "Ma changed the words!"

Every head in the room bent closer, as they tried to hear.

" . . . and I . . . am . . . almost . . . ho-ome . . . .
Lead Thou . . . me . . . on . . . ."

Louisa stopped, and for a moment they thought she had gone from them.

She had not. There were things she planned to say first.

"Gayle." Louisa opened her eyes and looked straight at him. Even without the crooking of her forefinger, the way she said it made him know he was to go to her. Wallace stepped back to make room for him close by the bed.

For the last time in her life, Louisa's voice became firm. She knew what she knew, and she was about to tell it to someone she loved. It was very important.

"Gayle," she said again, "you stay close to the Lord. Don't go back to your own ideas and go wandering off and away from him. Don't go back to thinking you are such a big man you've got to rely on yourself. You'll always need him—even more than you understand yet!"

"Besides . . . ," she softened the words with a smile, "I want to see you again. I don't want to get to heaven and find out you aren't coming."

Gayle could say nothing. Words couldn't get past the lump in his throat, but he ducked his head and nodded.

It was funny, really. If anyone else in any other circumstances had talked to Gayle like that—as if he were a little kid about to run away from home, a little kid who had to be scolded into behaving—he might have been offended.

But it wasn't anybody else who said it. It was Louisa, who was dying, and who spoke from a heart filled with love for him—so much love that she was willing to risk offending him in order to leave with him those final, important words.

Gayle could put up with a lot worse for so much love. At a time like this, instead of offending him, the scolding moved him close to tears. A knot of muscles along his jawline worked hard. Then he bent and kissed her.

"Even heaven," Louisa continued, "might be a little lonely without you."

Her gaze widened, at that, to include the others.

This was the moment, then, for her last good-bys to her children.

The thought struck Louisa that it would be nice to say good-by to places, too: the house on Monroe Street, the log cabin where Wallace had been born, the covered bridge over Riley Creek, the little white frame Missionary Church, the old red barn where she had first heard Chris praying for her, even the corner grocery store. There was no time for that. Besides, most of those places were gone now.

"Good-by, Wallace," she said.

"Good-by, Mary." Her eyes settled on each of them one last time, as they seemed to grow dim and fade from sight.

"Good-by, Norma . . . Gayle . . . Teri . . . Jennie . . . ."

Their tears troubled her. "Don't cry for me," she told them. "Death is not an awesome thing . . . not for those who go . . . only for those who stay behind."

"Don't cry for me," she said again. "I'm only going home."

While the rest of them wept, Louisa slipped quietly away from them and went her way rejoicing.

"Hold my hand, please," was the last thing she said.

The watchers at her bedside looked from face to face—and realized she wasn't talking to any of them.